David Scott has written several successful cookery books, among them *The Japanese Cookbook*, *Middle-Eastern Vegetarian Cookery* and *Indonesian Cookery*. He spent a year in Japan studying cookery and Uechi-Ryu karate and has visited and explored the cuisines of many countries, particularly in the East.

Paddy Byrne, restaurateur/chef at the Everyman Bistro, has since the age of 16 travelled extensively in Europe, North Africa and the USA, studying the movement of culinary ideas from one culture to another. He also has an expert knowledge of the British wholesale fruit and vegetable trade.

The authors are co-proprietors of the Everyman Bistro in Liverpool.

Also by David Scott

The Japanese Cookbook
Middle-Eastern Vegetarian Cookery
Indonesian Cookery

PADDY BYRNE
& DAVID SCOTT

Seasonal Salads

GRAFTON BOOKS

A Division of the Collins Publishing Group

LONDON GLASGOW
TORONTO SYDNEY AUCKLAND

Grafton Books
A Division of the Collins Publishing Group
8 Grafton Street, London W1X 3LA

Published by Grafton Books 1990

First published in Great Britain by
Ebury Press 1985

A CIP catalogue record for this book
is available from the British Library

ISBN 0-586-20811-9

Printed and bound in Great Britain by
Collins, Glasgow

Set in Garamond 3

CONTENTS

INTRODUCTION

The recipes in this book have been collected, adapted and devised by us over a period of 14 years. During this time we have bought produce for and operated a large popular restaurant that has established a fine reputation for its fresh salads. Our book contains ethnic recipes, classic combinations, many quite precise self-contained starter and side salads to accompany formal meals and a good number of novel, visually exciting, humorous even, but above all, fine-tasting salads that you will not have found elsewhere.

By presenting the salads seasonally, we trust we will save you time and money searching the shops for a vegetable that is quite out of season or only to be had at great expense or well past its best.

With few exceptions the recipes are simple and we hope the book will provide a sound basis for your own creative salad making. It lays out the basic rules for producing delicious salads utilizing the great variety of colours, shapes, textures and tastes to be found in salad vegetables. The essence of the art of salad making is to really know the qualities of the raw materials, to judge how they can be best complemented and presented and to then compose the salad accordingly. This process is the heart of this book and we hope it will help you use your own creativity to produce a wide range of salads that do not just play a supporting role to fish or meat or cheese, but make an equal contribution to a meal.

Paddy Byrne and David Scott
Liverpool, December 1984

Salads and seasons

Outside the tropics all vegetables have their seasons.

Because it is central to the theme of the book, we must emphasize that, when we say a vegetable is in season, we do not just mean that it is available, but that it is at its tastiest and at its cheapest. This will probably be because it has been grown locally and will be both very fresh and plentiful. Prices will be further cut because costs of transport and packaging will be much reduced. So, by following our recipes season by season, you can save money on salad vegetables and, we hope, enjoy better, more nutritional salads. And always remember that in order to fully enjoy the variety of short-season vegetables you may sometimes have to push out into another season any produce that you know is available over a longer period. Our hints on buying salad vegetables on pages 13 to 30 will be particularly useful in this regard.

Dressings for salads

For most of our salads we have recommended a minimum quantity of dressing. This is for two reasons. Firstly, we are using vegetables when their flavour is at its finest and thus we want to complement the taste, not submerge it. Secondly, dressings usually contain oils and creams and though we would not do without them, we want to use these fat-rich ingredients in moderation. See pages 33 to 40 for recipes.

Always taste dressings before pouring them over the vegetables. You may like them a little sweeter or sharper or hotter than we do. Adjust them to your personal preferences since the recipes are certainly not sacrosanct. Another reason for tasting is that many ingredients are of variable strength, sweetness and flavour –

tomatoes, carrots, oranges, chillies, paprika, vinegars and, above all, shoyu sauce are all unpredictable and you should test each new ingredient before you begin to prepare your salad.

Garnishes

With thought and imagination garnishes can be improvised to reflect the content of the individual salads both visually and for flavour. To us, a garnish is an integral part of a salad and is much more than just a visual arrangement. There is nothing more boring than parsley scattered over everything. Sometimes, when the chosen vegetables are so carefully selected and cut that they look good from first to last mouthful, salads are best presented ungarnished.

Seasonal salads and vegetarians

All our recipes are vegetarian, yet the book is not for vegetarians alone. While many of the recipes will stand on their own they will all make excellent accompaniments to every kind of meat, fish, egg and cheese dish.

Seasonal salads and the health-conscious

Most of our recipes could form part of a healthy, high-fibre, low-fat diet. Those few recipes with a high fat content are frequently accompanied by suggestions for low-fat alternatives. Conversely, some recipes low in fat may have suggestions to make them more appealing to those who like a richer diet. Nobody continues to eat food they dislike. People eating and enjoying their vegetables will gradually evolve a healthier diet.

General guidelines for salad making

● Use only the very best and freshest ingredients.

● Be selective about what goes into a salad: a thoughtless collection of vegetables will appeal to neither the tongue nor the eye. A great many salads are spoilt by the introduction of extra ingredients. Add nothing without considering how it will affect the final taste and appearance of the salad.

● Do not roughly chop up all salad ingredients similarly. Respect the characteristic shape of each vegetable and how it is seen to its best advantage. This may mean cutting cabbage into long corrugated strips, peppers into their sectional rings, horizontally cutting beef tomatoes to show off their wonderful 'map-of-the-world' cross-section, or leaving thin, twig-like French beans uncut. If you have several salads to prepare, see that you cut each in a different manner. Indeed if you are presenting a large buffet, prepare some salads by hand and some by machine to give even greater visual variety.

● Remember that strong-tasting vegetables such as garlic or onions used in small quantities as flavourings should be chopped up very finely in order to distribute their flavour evenly. Similarly, large, bland, starchy vegetables such as potatoes should be cut or sliced small to enable the dressing to penetrate easily.

● Beware unhappy combinations, in which colours clash horribly (for example, tomato and beetroot, or radish and radicchio). Don't mix ingredients such as celery and fennel which look alike and crunch in a similar manner or the effect on the taste buds will be reminiscent of tasting coffee when you thought you were about to taste tea. Beans, lentils and other starchy foods are usually best served as separate salads, as they muddy the clean taste of many more delicate ingredients.

● Many salads are valued for their crisp textures and sharp colours. So it is essential that ingredients are not overcooked and that any green vegetables, once cooked, are quickly chilled under running or iced water to arrest the cooking process and preserve their texture and colour.

● Season and mix salads adequately, although in the light of recent findings it may be wise to use salt with discretion. Those who salt their cooked meals well will obviously not enjoy unsalted salads. Cabbage, dried beans, lentils and, of course, potatoes, all need more salt than most vegetables. Pulses need plenty of vinaigrette to give an edge to their earthy taste.

● Match dressings and solid ingredients carefully. For instance, a subtle dressing will be lost over a coarse-flavoured pulse or sharply flavoured endive, while strong dressings would swamp a delicate salad of lettuce or fresh, immature broad beans.

● Don't add too many different fresh herbs to your salads. All you are likely to do is to overload and confuse the palate.

USEFUL KITCHEN EQUIPMENT

The great majority of salads can be prepared using a minimum of good-quality kitchen equipment. One good, sharp knife is worth more than a rackful of inferior, blunt ones. With that premise in mind here are a few comments on some of the equipment we have found essential or very useful in our kitchens and at home.

Blenders Electric blenders are extremely useful; with them dressings can be made in seconds and the preparation time of many dishes is radically reduced.

Chopping boards A chopping board is essential for convenience, accident-free cutting, protecting kitchen surfaces and extending the life of the cutting edges of knives. Hard woods such as maple or sycamore are good, but the health authorities now frown on the use of any porous materials and recommend the new polypropylene boards. Whichever material you choose, keep the board spotless. Use a sanitizer or scald the board frequently to kill off any bacteria it may harbour.

Cookware If you can afford stainless steel cookware, buy it. Stainless steel is robust and very easy to clean. Enamelware is equally good for cooking, but it will chip, leaving the base iron exposed. Even the enamelled cast ironware will eventually wear out. Aluminium or uncoated ironware taints or discolours many vegetables and sauces. Forget about non-stick pans: the coating seldom remains intact for long and you're then left with a thin inferior aluminium pan.

Food mixer Whisking up mayonnaise in a food mixer is very easy. If you do a lot of baking as well as salad making a food mixer with a grating/slicing attachment may be a better combination tool for you than a food processor.

Food processors A food processor does most of the tasks a blender does. It will also grate and slice vegetables. This is a very useful asset if you wish to produce economical salads in winter and early spring. If you make lots of soups as well as salads this would be your ideal kitchen aid. Good ones are expensive.

Garlic press Buy a large garlic press so that the cloves are more likely to be squeezed through the grid rather than out round the edges of the press. Also useful for juicing fresh ginger and fresh chillies.

Jelly bag A traditional jelly bag is ideal for straining excess liquid from overwatery yoghurt. A piece of muslin makes a good substitute.

Knife sharpener A steel knife sharpener or oilstone (best of all for stainless steel knives) is a must. There is nothing more time-consuming or frustrating than working with a blunt knife. Blunt knives are more likely to slip and cause accidents as you have to use so much more force behind them than would be necessary if the cutting edge was sharp.

If you are on very good terms with your butcher or fishmonger he may sharpen or even regrind your knives when necessary.

Knives Two knives will be sufficient: a medium cook's knife and a small paring knife. Although they are much more difficult to sharpen, we prefer stainless steel knives. Carbon steel taints or blackens many foods, such as aubergines, avocados, globe artichokes, red cabbage and most fruit. Many people would also use a small serrated-edged knife, but these cannot be resharpened.

Lemon juicer We have found that the traditional hand-held, carved wooden lemon juicer is the best and simplest tool for extracting small quantities of citrus juices.

Mortar and pestle We hope you will buy your spices whole, that is, in their natural state. You will then need a mortar and pestle to pound and pulverize these seeds and pods. Buy a mortar with deep vertical sides to prevent the seeds from shooting out all over the kitchen.

Peeler With a little practice the swivel-bladed vegetable peeler is quicker to use and less wasteful than our traditional fixed-blade potato peeler.

Pepper grinder Absolutely essential; wherever we say 'black pepper to taste', we mean freshly ground. Also useful for other spices such as coriander.

Scissors Scissors are the best tool for trimming fresh herbs and topping and tailing French beans and mangetout peas.

Wire whisk Choose a good, traditional wire whisk that feels comfortable in the hand and you will quickly develop a skill with it. Stainless steel is again preferred, as tin whisks are rapidly attacked by and will taint acidic dressings.

Other equipment Other useful items not mentioned here would include colanders and sieves, a hand or rotary grater, measuring jugs and spoons, mixing bowls, a salad spinner, small scales and wooden spoons.

OILS AND VINEGARS

Well-flavoured oils and vinegars are essential for making attractive, tasty salads. They provide their own taste and are the base for any additional flavourings such as herbs or spices. Salad dressings demand a better quality of oil than you might use for cooking. Unrefined oils should be chosen in preference to the cheaper, refined oils where the extraction process is to the detriment of flavour and is aided by the application of heat and chemicals rather than a purely mechanical pressing. The strong flavours of unrefined oils can, if necessary, be toned down by the addition of some neutral-tasting oil.

The strongly flavoured oils

Olive oil   It is better to use a good olive oil with discretion than a poor one continuously. Good olive oil has a clean, fruity flavour without any aftertaste. The lighter French and Italian olive oils are the most easily digested of all the cooking oils. The thick fruity oils from Greece and Spain are less easily digested. Try a bottle from each country in turn and discover as you would with wines which flavours and characteristics you prefer. We would advise you to buy Extra Virgin or Virgin Fine oil that has come from the first or cold pressing of the olives. Reserve your very best olive oil for leaf salads. They require so little vinaigrette that the extra cost of using even the most expensive olive oil on them is small.

Although we have tried a wide range of olive oils in the restaurant, mayonnaise made from them has seldom been as well received as mayonnaise from the more neutral oils. This is our own experience too, working with an even wider range of olive oils; but we must confess that we have had excellent olive-oil-based mayon-naise in certain restaurants in France. Olive oil neither adds to nor reduces cholesterol levels in the blood.

Sesame oil   A sweet nutty-flavoured oil, very good in association with shoyu sauce or for cooking aubergines. Buy the thick, brownish non-refined oil.

Walnut oil   An alternative to olive oil on the more robust green leaf salads. A strong nutty taste not to everyone's liking. Does not keep well, buy in small amounts and keep in a cool place.

The neutral oils

By definition, these are going to be generally quite similar, though different brands of the same oil may taste different. Some will be clean-tasting, others will have a considerable aftertaste. Try several and when you find the brand you like, stick to it.

Corn oil   The label may say it's good for salads, several books may agree, but we have always found it heavy and flat. Keep it for frying.

Groundnut oil   Much recommended by the prophets of the 'new cuisine'. Good examples have a light, mild flavour. Unfortunately there seems to be a lot of inferior oil about. Also known as peanut or arachide oil.

Safflower oil   The ideal oil for anyone on a low-fat diet, for it is very high in polyunsaturates. Now found only in whole- or health-food shops; expensive.

Soya oil   We find this oil pleasant to use; though it is often said to have a strong aftertaste, we have not found this so.

Sunflower oil   A thin, mild oil high in polyunsaturates. Add a little olive oil if you want more flavour.

Vinegars

We could have suggested that you use rice vinegar in one recipe, sherry vinegar in another, wine vinegar in this and cider vinegar in that, but then your cupboards would soon be full of seldom-used bottles. We use an organically produced cider vinegar in most of our recipes. A good wine vinegar produced by the Orléans method would be a splendid but more expensive alternative. It is more important that you have one good vinegar than a selection of inferior ones. This does not mean that you should only ever use one sort of vinegar – if you like a certain specialist vinegar, keep that as well. Avoid malt vinegar and distilled spirit vinegars.

You can produce your own flavoured vinegars by infusing fresh herbs like marjoram, rosemary, tarragon or thyme for at least a week in small bottles of vinegar.

BUYING, PREPARING AND COOKING FRESH FRUIT AND VEGETABLES

Apples   Our native fruit is extremely good. Outside their natural season, you will pay more for apples that have been stored too long. Each variety of apple is at its best and cheapest for a relatively short period. Here are some suggestions: late summer, George Cave; early autumn, James Grieve; late autumn, Worcester Pearmain; winter, Cox's Orange Pippin; and late winter, Winston.

Artichokes, globe   Globe artichokes are most widely available in late spring and early summer. They should be green and crisp, without any withered leaves. Choose leafy compact specimens whose outer leaves are fleshy.

Soak the artichokes upside-down for an hour in salted water to drive out any hidden insects. Pull or cut away, with a sharp stainless steel knife, any damaged outer leaves and break off the stem; rub cut surfaces with lemon juice. Plunge each prepared artichoke immediately into a bowl of acidulated water.

When all the artichokes are prepared, swiftly drain them and drop them into rapidly boiling, salted and acidulated water in a stainless steel or enamel pan. Cook at a gentle boil for 20–35 minutes, according to their size. Pull off an outer leaf and test for tenderness. Stand them upside-down to drain.

Asparagus   The short asparagus season runs from late spring to early summer. Choose asparagus with tight heads and, as freshness is all important, check that they have been recently cut by examining the severed stem. Generally, the thicker the shoots the more expensive asparagus is. Particularly good value are the long, thin stalks of asparagus (often called sprue) whose heads can be broken off just above their lower stringy section. Thicker asparagus will need its coarse skin peeling off to expose the tender middle.

Tie the asparagus into individual serving-sized bundles. Stand them, heads up, in a saucepan and cook them in gently boiling, salted water for 5–15 minutes, according to the thickness of the stems. The heads themselves should steam above the level of the water. Take great care not to overcook.

Aubergines   Though available to us for most of the year, we believe that (as with tomatoes) during our cooler seasons aubergines have more flavour when grown in warmer countries where they can prosper without too much artificial feeding and protection. The small, irregular aubergines air-freighted to us from Kenya are the best-flavoured. Choose glossy, firm unblemished specimens with, most importantly, good fresh stems. Reject any aubergines without stems as the retailer may have removed the stems when they began to wither or go mouldy. If possible, always use plastic, stainless steel or enamel implements when preparing and cooking aubergines as they blacken on contact with carbon steel or aluminium.

Aubergines may be sliced and salted and left lightly pressed to drain in a colander for 30 minutes or more to draw off some of their slightly bitter juices. This also reduces the amount of oil they absorb whilst being fried. Rather than frying or steaming sliced or cubed aubergines we have been baking whole aubergines in a very hot oven for about fifteen minutes or until the skin turns crisp. Remove the aubergines from the oven and quickly peel off the skin. This is hot on the fingers, but otherwise a simple operation. Beware of overbaking the aubergines or they may explode.

Avocados   These are at their best and cheapest between late autumn and early spring. Hass avocados, those alligator-skinned fruits from Israel available in late winter and early spring, are to be recommended. We have been very disappointed in the flavour of summer avocados with the exception of the expensive Californian varieties. Like other fruit, avocados can only be enjoyed when they are properly ripe. They should be soft and 'give' when touched, particularly around the neck. Buy avocados unripe and store them in a warm room until they reach this condition. The skins can be quite black before the flesh is overripe; however, fruit with cracked, sunken or badly bruised skins are usually beyond redemption. Use stainless steel knives to cut the flesh and brush any stored avocado halves or pieces with lemon juice to retard the blackening process.

To halve avocados make a deep encircling cut from the neck down to the base and back up to the neck. Give the avocado a sharp twist and lift away the free half. Still holding in the palm of your hand the avocado half with the stone embedded in it, lightly chop at the stone with your sharp knife so that the blade is held by the stone. Give the knife a sharp twist and the stone will come away on the knife blade. To remove the avocado skin prior to slicing or dicing the flesh, lay the halves skin up on a chopping board and make several shallow cuts from the neck to the base. The skin can then be peeled off in segments. Half-avocados can be prevented from discolouring for twelve hours or more by leaving the stone in and rubbing the exposed cut surface liberally with olive oil before wrapping closely with clingfilm and storing in the fridge.

Beansprouts   Available all the year round, these are very useful as a crisp, light component of winter salads. They can be bought in many supermarkets, but they are exceptionally cheap if bought from a Chinese provision merchant. To prepare beansprouts just wash them and drain them thoroughly.

Beetroot   Best in early summer when they are small, sweet and tender. They are available until the following spring, but will become progressively woodier, so unless you are particularly fond of beetroot, avoid them after mid-winter.

Beetroot can be grated and eaten raw but most people prefer them cooked. Cook them in boiling water; they are ready as soon as the skin will rub off – 15–45 minutes according to age and size. Never cut beetroot before cooking them; just twist the tops off, otherwise you will lose most of the colour and flavour.

Broad beans   These are among the first vegetables of the new season. If you can grow them yourself, pick them small and eat them raw with just a scattering of sea-salt for a real treat.

Most bought broad beans are over-mature and will need cooking. Use a minimum of slightly salted, boiling water and cook until tender. If they are not tender after eight minutes, make a soup out of them.

Broccoli   There are several types. Home-grown *sprouting broccoli* is available from late winter to early spring, in both purple and white forms. It is usually inexpensive, but the season is very short and dependent on weather conditions. Sprouting broccoli is very tasty with a strong flavour, but it does break up easily. It is excellent eaten on its own, like asparagus; don't toss it with other ingredients – it will just turn to a mush. For preparation and cooking see below.

Calabrese or *green broccoli*. Imported most of the year round, from Spain and Israel. Excellent local-grown calabrese is in season from mid-summer to early autumn. Calabrese (Calabria is the southernmost region of Italy) arrives here during spring and autumn, but oddly enough, we have found the Italian produce far from satisfactory – a large tough wooden stem and a flower head that overcooks and becomes sodden too easily.

Calabrese must be fresh. Only buy it when it has its distinctive bright mid-green colour. Avoid any heads that show signs of the yellowing flowers which are beginning to burst. We avoid imported calabrese in summer as it deteriorates so quickly in the heat. If buying pre-packed broccoli, select bundles with stems of similar thickness so they cook evenly.

To prepare *purple* or *white sprouting broccoli*, pull off any coarse leaves and trim back coarse stalks. To prepare *green broccoli* or *calabrese*, trim base of stalk, peel the tough skin off the stalk back to the flower head and finally, should the stalks be thick, cut them lengthways once or twice as necessary, so that the stalk will cook as rapidly as the flower head.

Cook all broccoli stalk-down in 2–3 cm (1 in) of very rapidly boiling salted water for 5–8 minutes until tender (squeeze the stalk to test). Gently drain the broccoli and if it is to be served cold, chill it rapidly in iced water or under cold running water.

Cabbages   Red and white drumhead cabbages are available to us all year round, but between mid-spring and late summer they are expensive. Savoy cabbages are plentiful from late autumn to early spring.

When preparing cabbages, cut away the coarse ribs and the central core. Try to cut the cabbage into thin strips in such a way that its wavy corrugated leaves are seen to full advantage.

Carrots   It's fair to say that we grow better carrots than anyone else. They are delicious in early summer and are good until mid-winter, after which they become progressively tougher and more expensive. Imported new-season carrots reach us in early spring, first from Cyprus, then from Italy and then from southern France, but they are never very juicy.

The early spring English finger carrots can just be brushed clean. Later on in the season they need peeling, otherwise the skin darkens and looks unappetizing.

Cauliflowers   Like all vegetables, cauliflowers are expensive in early spring. Outside that period their price varies enormously, since storage is a problem. Once cauliflowers are ready for picking they don't keep well on the plant, nor do they keep well once cut. The result is that sometimes the wholesale markets have too many cauliflowers and they are cheap, and sometimes they don't have enough to go around and they are expensive. The moral of the story is buy cauliflowers when they are cheap and ignore them when they are expensive. A cauliflower's face is its fortune: if it looks good it will taste good. Choose heavy, white, unpitted heads.

Experiment using cauliflower raw; it has a wonderful crunchy texture. Never use overcooked cauliflower in salads. It is best steamed or par-boiled in 2–4 cm (1–2 in) of slightly salted boiling water. The florets will be cooked in 5 minutes while the whole heads will take a little more than 15 minutes. Chill the cooked cauliflower in the usual manner to prevent overcooking.

Celeriac   Also known as bulb or root celery, celeriac is much neglected in this country – a great pity, for it has a very fine flavour. Start looking for it in early autumn. It looks like a small swede with a wrinkled skin. Celeriac for salads, diced, sliced or cut in julienne, is often blanched by dropping it in boiling water for one minute. Drain the celeriac well before dressing. Choose regular-looking roots which are heavy for their size; they should not have too many deep crevices or bulbous swellings; avoid any celeriac with soft brown patches.

Once celeriac has been peeled and cut, it must be placed immediately in acidulated water [30 ml (2 tablespoons) vinegar per litre (2 pints)] or it will have discoloured before you have a chance to put the dressing on.

Celery   Available to us the whole year round imported from Spain or Israel but at its cheapest when home-grown is on the market, from early summer to mid-winter. The summer green or self-blanching celery looks best but the white, blanched, autumn and winter celery has the best flavour.

Avoid putting all but a few celery leaves in a salad, they are just too bitter.

Courgettes   Throughout summer local courgettes are cheap and plentiful. The season for the more expensive Mediterranean-grown varieties begins earlier and extends well into the autumn, while the still more expensive, air-freighted Kenyan courgettes are available during the close season of the Mediterranean imports. Late season British and Mediterranean courgettes are best avoided for they often have a poor, slightly acrid taste, probably because of the slower growth. Choose courgettes no longer than 15 cm (6 in) with tight, unblemished skins. The yellow variety look tremendous in salads.

Cook courgettes whole in boiling, salted water for 5 minutes or until they just 'give' a little when gently squeezed. Rapidly chill them in the usual manner. Top and tail the cooked courgettes and slice them into 1 cm (⅜ in) sections. Courgettes to be fried should be cut in a similar manner, placed in a colander, sprinkled with salt and left, lightly pressed, to drain for an hour. Rinse and dry the slices before frying them. Courgettes can also be served raw, sliced wafer-thin, although we usually steam them for 2 minutes to make them more digestible.

Cucumbers   Available all year round, these are at their best and cheapest during the hotter months. If they are expensive use alternative salad ingredients. Choose firm, dark green fruit and avoid any which are large or over-bloated. Whether you peel cucumbers or leave them intact is usually a matter of personal taste. It is, however, a good idea to reduce the water content in cucumbers by placing the sliced or diced fruit in a colander, sprinkling it with salt and leaving it lightly pressed to drain for at least half an hour. The cucumber need not be rinsed after this operation as the salt will drain away with the water (you will probably not need to resalt the salad). The water content can be further reduced by cutting the whole fruit in half lengthwise and removing the watery seeds by running the back of a teaspoon firmly along the seed channel. Slice the cucumber and salt as described.

Dried beans, chickpeas and lentils   All these pulses first need careful checking and rinsing to remove stones and other foreign bodies. All but the lentils are best left soaking overnight. Dried beans absorb a great deal of water and they will more than double their weight, so it is important to cover all the beans with enough water so they will still be submerged the following morning. Drain the beans, place them in a pan and re-cover with fresh, *unsalted* water. Bring the beans to the boil, cook over a brisk heat for 5 minutes, cover the pan and reduce to a simmer. The beans will probably take nearly an hour to cook, but check them after half an hour and then every 10 minutes, adding a little water if necessary. Salt the beans just 5–10 minutes before you think they will be cooked. Drain but do not rinse the cooked beans. Although it is not essential we think that the pulses are best cooked with flavourings such as a carrot, half an onion and a bouquet garni containing a sprig of thyme, a bay leaf, parsley stalks and a celery stalk or lovage.

Green beans   French and runner beans are the two main types but new varieties are being tested in the marketplace every year. Most successful of these is the broad, flat-podded kwintos bean that arrives in spring from Spain and later from Guernsey. Tastiest of all the recent vegetable introductions is the snap pea, which is very expensive in the shops but simple to grow yourself. We have included it here because the whole pod is eaten and they are prepared and cooked as French beans.

The season and sources of the *French beans* are similar to those of the courgette. Likewise, they are best eaten small. When you are buying French beans check that they are of equal size and maturity; many local growers grade very badly.

Top and tail the beans and drop them into a pan of rapidly boiling salted water and cook, uncovered, over a brisk heat until barely tender (4–8 minutes). For use in salads, drain the beans immediately and plunge them into iced water or cool under cold running water.

Runner beans are a British favourite and always (we think) locally grown. New stringless varieties are being introduced, but it seems that most cooks' ideas of stringless and the growers' are not quite the same thing. Perhaps the beans are just allowed to grow too large, so that the growers obtain a heavier crop (and more money – a shame). Choose the smaller, smooth, even-sized, bright green pods.

Top and tail runner beans and remove with a vegetable peeler any stringy bits from either edge, although hopefully there won't be any. Don't cut the pods up before you cook them or you will lose so much flavour. At the most cut them in half to get them into the pan. For use in salads, cook and cool the runner beans in a similar manner to French beans. They will take 8–12 minutes to reach tenderness. Cut the cold pods into small, diagonal sections.

Fennel Bulb or Italian Florence fennel is at its best in summer but it is often overlooked because there is such a choice of vegetables at that time. Local bulb fennel available in late summer and early autumn is seldom cheaper than the imported produce. Fennel remains available throughout autumn and winter and, although it makes a refreshing change during the later part of the year, its quality progressively diminishes. Choose firm, unwithered bulbs free of blemishes.

Prepare the fennel for salads by removing any tough lower stalks or outer skins and cut out the solid centre core. Slice the prepared bulb as desired.

Garlic This is available throughout the year but in late spring and early summer, before the new crop arrives, it is always in poor shape. At that time of the year choose very carefully; reject light or mouldy bulbs, but don't blame your greengrocer for them. Await the new crop, especially the thick-necked wet garlic from Provence. Take great care when frying garlic because it burns very quickly.

Grapefruit Another Mediterranean fruit; like oranges, they are in season in winter and early spring, but available at a premium from other parts of the world throughout the year.

Leaf vegetables, see page 26.

Leeks In late spring and early summer look out for the delicious, tiny, finger-thick leeks. In late autumn, winter and early spring, the white and very pale green parts of mature leeks, sliced very finely, can be used in many salads to replace onions.

To prepare tiny leeks, cut off the roots, trim back the green tops and remove any damaged outer layers. Make a deep vertical cut down through the green top into the white section and wash the leaves thoroughly under the tap to remove any soil. Prepare mature leeks for salads by cutting off the roots and green tops and finely slicing the white stem into rounds. Place the rounds in a colander, press them out into rings and wash well.

Lemons   They come from the same countries as oranges. Though available all year round, they are more expensive outside the main autumn and winter season.

Limes   These tropical fruits reach us from many sources. Available all year round at a fairly constant price, in late summer they are often cheaper than lemons. Some are very sharp.

Mangetout (snow or sugar) peas   Mangetout are delicious; they bring the freshness of early summer to our dark winter and early spring days. They are always expensive. Take care when you buy mangetout because far too many are on sale that are grossly over-mature. The pods must be quite flat, the tiny peas registering no more than a dot in their bright green overcoats. If this is not the case you are only buying disappointment.

Prepare the pods by snapping off the stalk and pulling it backwards towards the tip to remove the coarse thread. Snap off the top and pull that backwards towards the stalk end to remove the remaining coarse thread. Cook as for French beans (page 20).

Mushrooms   Available throughout the year, though slightly cheaper in summer. Mushrooms are scarce during sudden cold periods. Only the fresh, closed, white, button mushrooms should be used in salads. They can be served raw, finely sliced and dressed with lemon juice or a herb-flavoured vinaigrette.

Onions, spring onions and shallots   While mature onions are obviously available all the year round, they reach us from many parts of the world and exhibit very different characteristics. Always taste a small piece of the onion before deciding how much to put in a salad. If it tastes extremely harsh, reduce the quantity used or replace it with a milder spring onion or shallot. We do recommend the sweet mid-summer Spanish onion for salads.

Outside Britain, spring onions are used far more freely – in Creole cooking, for example, they are used almost to the exclusion of mature onions. Try finely sliced larger spring onion in salads.

In late summer and early autumn when the new-season shallots are first available they may seem very expensive, but try asking your greengrocer for a small net of them. Hang this in a dry, airy place, and use the delicately flavoured, aromatic bulbs all winter and on into early spring.

Oranges   These are cheapest in late winter and throughout spring. They come from the whole Mediterranean area: Greece, Turkey, Cyprus, Spain and Israel.

Pears   These like slightly warmer conditions than apples and though we grow our own, some of the best pears come from countries just to the south of us. The season begins and ends with Italian pears: the Williams in mid-summer and the Passacrassana as late as spring. English William pears begin in early autumn and are followed by Beurre Hardy in mid-autumn and by Conference and Comice in late autumn. The natural season is extended by retarding ripening in cool storage which causes loss of flavour.

Peas   Unless you grow them yourself, fresh garden peas are a thing of the past. You can buy peas in the pod but in our experience they will contain as many coarse, overripe starch-laden peas as young fresh green peas.

Peppers, sweet (capsicums)   Available all the year round from a variety of sources. Green peppers are at their cheapest from mid-summer to mid-autumn. Red peppers are usually more expensive than green, though in spring there are abundant supplies of economically priced red and yellow peppers from the Canaries.

To prepare raw peppers, remove the stem and seed cluster and remove loose seeds. Intense direct heat transforms peppers. They develop a deep, rich, sweet flavour and a soft, velvety texture. Red or yellow peppers are superb prepared this way. The simplest method is to cut the peppers in half, remove the seeds and brush both sides with oil. Lay cut side down on a baking tray and place in a preheated oven at 240°C (475°F, Gas Mark 9) until the skins are loose and puckered. The skins can then be easily removed from the hot peppers. A more smoky flavour is attained if the peppers are roasted whole over a gas or charcoal flame or under the hottest preheated grill, turning them until the skin is charred all over. The removal of the skin is more painstaking than before, and the debris may need to be rinsed away under cold running water. Try not to lose the tasty juices from within the peppers.

Peppers, hot (chillies)   There are nearly 100 types of hot chilli peppers in use in Mexico, three, four or more different ones being used in the preparation of just one dish. Here we may see a maximum of five different varieties in the whole year. The best and the easiest to use is the *jalapeño* or bullet pepper imported from Kenya for most of the year, but available from British growers in late summer and autumn. They are very hot, so you only need buy them in small quantities. Add less than the recommended amount of chillies until you discover how hot they are.

To prepare chillies, cut off the stalks, slit the bodies of the chillies open, remove and discard the seeds (although in Mexico they would not be wasted). Do not rub your eyes or face and wash your hands immediately you have finished handling them.

Pineapples   In season for most of the year, slightly more expensive in early and mid-autumn before the main South African season begins. In salads, tinned fruit is a poor substitute for the real thing.

Pomegranates   A fun fruit only available in autumn, generally from Spain. The beautiful red, bitter-sweet seeds are more than just a garnish when added to crisp leaf or fruit salads.

Potatoes   Until recently if you wanted the special firm salad potatoes such as Pink Fir Apple or Red Cardinal you would have had to grow them yourself. These and other similar varieties are now on sale at some of the more progressive supermarkets. They are expensive and still worth growing yourself. There has been a change in taste away from soft, white-fleshed potatoes to firmer fleshed varieties that are all quite good in salads. Maris Bard, Maris Peer, Desiree and the old Arran Pilot are all satisfactory and quite easy to obtain. If you are prepared to pay, you can have new potatoes from just before Christmas when the traditional Italian new potatoes arrive. These are followed by new potatoes from Morocco, Egypt, the Canaries and then in early spring, expensive and, we think, disappointing, Jersey Royals. In our view the potatoes from the Canaries are the best for the price. Look out for the little 'mid' potatoes.

New potatoes should just be washed and brushed clean. Trim off any green or damaged areas. Clean and trim older potatoes in a similar manner. Cook potatoes in boiling, salted water, in their skins. For salads, remove the skins while the potatoes are still warm, sometimes they will just pull off. Remember to cut large potatoes into easy-to-eat pieces before you pour on the dressing.

Radishes   Radishes are at their best in late spring and early summer when, with the soil and the sun getting warmer every day, they grow fast and furiously, producing succulent, crisp, peppery roots. Once the summer sun has dried the ground out the roots are never so tender. We think it is better to use the large white radish (also called daikon or mooli) from late summer onwards. When buying our traditional red radish, look for firm, bright, unblemished roots with good fresh dark green leaves still attached. Avoid oversized roots, they will be hollow and bitter-fleshed. When choosing daikon, pick roots about 2.5 cm (1 in) thick.

Sweetcorn   We confess that we have used tinned sweetcorn for most of the recipes in this book. We do use fresh corn in late summer and the first two weeks of autumn when heads of local sweetcorn can be bought cheaply. It must be very fresh since, once cut, sweetcorn rapidly loses its flavour. In this country we don't eat enough corn to have learned how to pick it at its best. It is invariably sold overripe.

Choose bright green husks with pale brown silks and plump creamy yellow kernels. (It will not matter if the kernels at the very top are not yet mature.) Husk the corn and drop it into a pan of rapidly boiling, *unsalted* water. The corn will be cooked 2–3 minutes after the water has returned to the boil. For use in salads, cool the corn heads, hold them vertically on a chopping board and cut off the kernels with a sharp knife.

Tomatoes   Trying to buy tasty tomatoes is a bit like trying to follow a treasure trail. Here are some clues to help you towards the goal.

In cold seasons buy tomatoes from the warmer, sunnier growing areas since tomatoes prosper in the sun. In high season, buy local tomatoes that have not yet lost the smell of the tomato plant. Whatever the season, look out for the high-flavoured varieties such as the Tiny Cherry or Gardener's Delight tomatoes from Britain in middle and late summer; the plum tomatoes from Italy in mid-summer; the beef tomatoes from Spain or anywhere but Holland. Canary tomatoes are usually well flavoured and we think the flavour of Spanish tomatoes has improved in the last few years. Sadly, plant breeders in some countries seem more concerned with the genes that produce even-sized fruit than the genes that produce the flavour.

To skin tomatoes, bring a medium-sized pan of water to the boil. Take the tomatoes and, with a sharp pointed knife, remove the stalk and that hard little section of flesh the stalk is attached to. Drop the tomatoes one or two at a time into the boiling water for several seconds. Remove them with a slotted spoon and cool them under cold water. The tomato skin will easily peel or even fall off. Remove excess liquid and seeds from tomatoes by cutting them in half horizontally and gently squeezing and shaking the liquid out.

Leaf vegetables

Home-grown leaf salads   If you want a green leaf salad, or just a light crisp salad in winter or early spring, there is plenty of choice, but you may have to pay a little extra. Into your cold season salad bowl goes imported Cos or Iceberg lettuce, the chicories and endives, Chinese cabbage, beansprouts, dandelion leaves, newly sprouted sorrel, spinach and watercress.

While it is fairly obvious when these leaf vegetables are in good condition, remember the following points:

● Clean, neat lettuces in little polythene bags will almost certainly be less tasty than the big, untrimmed specimens with soil still on their outer leaves.

● Check, particularly with Cos lettuce, that they have not begun to bolt. If they have, the leaves will be bitter, not sweet.

● Variety is very important in leaf salads. Buy several sorts to use together and keep them wrapped in damp newspapers in the bottom of the refrigerator.

Hints for preparing leaf vegetables

1. Nearly all the leaf vegetables are very fragile, so handle them with care when stripping the plants down, when washing and drying the leaves and when tossing the completed salad.
2. Drain and shake the leaves dry. Don't serve salads with a puddle underneath them. If you don't have a salad spinner use the old-fashioned method: place the washed leaves in a large, clean tea-towel, hold the four corners and swing the tea-towel in a lazy circle outside the back door.
3. It is unnecessary, indeed detrimental, to wash the extremely tightly packed hearts of chicory, iceberg lettuce, Chinese cabbage, and some varieties of Cos lettuce.
4. Unless you are going to use the leaf salad immediately, gently tear (don't cut) the leaves into smaller pieces. If you do cut the leaves you will find that they 'bleed' and collapse in a very short time. Moreover, cut leaves have a uniformity of shape we are seeking to avoid. Heavy ribbed leaves such as Cos lettuce can be cut along the rib without ill effect.

Dressing leaf salads

1. It is worth reserving your very best olive oil for your leaf salads. Curly endive and dandelion are best dressed with walnut oil, but use it on other leaf salads as well if you like its flavour. Make your dressing with a 4/1 or, if you are using just delicate leaves, a 5/1 oil/vinegar ratio.
2. Never dress your leaf salads until the very last moment, preferably at the table.
3. Toss your salad gently but thoroughly, scooping the leaves from the bottom of the heap to the top several times over.

Leaf vegetables for salads

Baak choi (tiny white Chinese cabbage) In season summer and early autumn, locally grown and inexpensive. Buy the smallest available, separate the leaves, wash well, dry and slice into small pieces.

Batavian endive In season winter and spring, imported from France and Italy, often inexpensive. Batavia looks like a slightly ragged lettuce. Prepare it as for lettuce; because of its bitter flavour it is best mixed with other greens.

Butterhead lettuce This is the common round variety we are most familiar with. Avoid the flopping winter and early spring maturing varieties. Fine in summer if you like a softer lettuce.

Chicory The pale green and white 'teeth' (*chicons*) of chicory make a very pleasant addition to our autumn, winter and early spring salads. This is a good salad standby as it keeps well if wrapped in cling film and placed in the refrigerator. Choose chicory whose leaves are tight, pointed and without any brown blemishes. The inner leaves are so closely packed that it is unnecessary to wash them. Chicory is less bitter than its cousin, the endive.

Chinese leaves (Peking cabbage) Available throughout the cold months when it is imported from Austria and Israel, although there are some inexpensive, locally grown Chinese leaves also on the market. This vegetable has much improved in quality over the last few years and the long, narrow variety is superior to the short, chunky type. When buying, check just inside the tip for brown rot. Remove any damaged outer leaves.

Cos lettuce Locally grown Cos is available throughout the summer and early autumn, while imported Cypriot, Israeli and Italian specimens are available in winter and early spring. Look out for a variety called Little Gem.

Curly endive This is imported from Provence in late autumn and early winter and again from Provence and Italy in early spring. Curly endive is usually quite expensive and looks like a riotous mop of ragged-edged leaves. Make sure when you buy that none of the leaves are slimy. Curly endive has a very bitter but refreshing taste. Serve in small quantities.

Dandelion This should be picked in early spring before it flowers. It can be very bitter, so use in small quantities.

Lamb's lettuce (corn salad) Delicious, dark green leaves the size and shape of a lamb's tongue, this is available from France in late autumn and in spring and erratically through the winter. It tends to be expensive but is well worthwhile for a special occasion.

Radicchio A round, beautiful deep red chicory with a white contrasting rib. Available from local growers during autumn and from Italy from autumn through to spring (but only erratically during the coldest months), radicchio is never cheap, whatever the source. It has quite a bitter taste. Buy just one head for its aesthetic value.

Rocket This has a powerful, fiery taste and is easily home-grown.

Sorrel See Summer Green Salad (page 66).

Spinach The fleshy, dark green leaves from young spinach plants are welcome additions to salads in spring and early summer.

True spinach, often known for obvious reasons as pink-footed spinach, is much superior to spinach beet leaves in all salads.

Watercress British-grown watercress is available at all times of the year except in the icy depths of winter. It is, we think, best avoided in winter and early spring, when the leaves are very small, and also when it is flowering, in mid-summer.

To prepare watercress for use, trim away the roots and wash thoroughly. Store, damp, in a sealed plastic container in the salad drawer of the refrigerator.

Webb and Iceberg lettuce Local Webb lettuces are available throughout summer and early autumn and new, hardier strains of Iceberg are now available from local growers until early winter. During the coldest months we have to rely on fairly expensive imports from Spain, Israel and even California. Iceberg lettuces have a fine, crisp texture but little flavour. Mix them with contrasting darker, tastier leaves. The hearts of these varieties are so tightly packed that it's best to cut them in half before pulling them apart.

Recent introductions

Suddenly there is a profusion of lettuce varieties to choose from. Look out for the following:

Lollo Red and Lollo Green The red variety is exceptionally handsome with attractive, frilled-edged leaves, but no great flavour.

Marvel of Four Seasons Red-leaved lettuce with delicate, curled leaves, a solid heart and good flavour.

Oakleaf lettuce Usually available in the bronze form. Large, fragile, beautifully curled and fringed leaves with a fine flavour.

THE ESSENTIAL STORE CUPBOARD

Few modern households have enough space for storing vast supplies of foodstuffs and for those which do there is always the danger that many ingredients would go to waste or grow stale before they were used. Our tip is to keep a small basic store cupboard of the best ingredients available, augment it with some personal favourites and extend its range by exploring one foreign cuisine at a time. If you find you dislike certain foreign foods, disregard them and their ingredients. You will probably never get to like them. Give any unwanted ingredients away at once or dispose of them since you do not want to have never-to-be-used materials cluttering up your kitchen. Kitchens are workshops and should be kept clear.

This is our selection of store cupboard ingredients. Those items in *italics* we consider essential, the others are recommended but open to personal taste.

Spices *Coriander, cumin, paprika, cayenne, sea salt, black pepper*, juniper, caraway, mustard seeds, white pepper, curry powder. See also pages 37 to 39.

Flavourings *Shoyu, sesame paste, hot pepper sauce*, shallots, *garlic*, fresh root ginger, mango chutney, peanut butter, coconut butter.

Oils *Olive oil, a neutral oil* (groundnut or sunflower), walnut oil, sesame oil.

Vinegars *Organic cider vinegar*, rice wine vinegar, red wine vinegar.

Herbs Grow as many fresh salad herbs as you can. We think only oregano and, perhaps, dill and mint are worth storing dried.

Tinned goods *Plum tomatoes*, sweetcorn.

Bottled or preserved goods *Olives*, pickled gherkins, horse radish sauce, *Dijon mustard*, Colman's English mustard powder.

Grains, beans and pulses   *Red kidney beans*, *haricot beans*, *chick peas*, large brown or green lentils, flageolet beans, bulgar wheat (burghul).

Dried pasta   Keep one of the short elbow, shell or twist shapes. A similar green pasta is attractive but not essential.

Nuts   None are essential, but walnuts and almonds and (to a lesser degree) hazelnuts are all useful.

Seeds   Again, none are essential, but both blue poppy seeds and the buff-coloured sesame seeds are very useful. Toasted sunflower seeds are a pleasant, nutritious addition to many salads.

Luxuries   Totally subjective, but ours would be cardamom seeds, pine nuts, pesto, pistachio nuts, tamarind seeds, limes in season.

Short-term store   The following are extremely handy to have in a short-term store: natural yoghurt, whipping cream, soured cream, fresh bean curd (tofu), fresh coconut, lemons.

HERBS, SPICES AND OTHER FLAVOURINGS FOR SALADS

Herbs

Robust herbs such as bay, thyme and rosemary retain some of their original flavour even when dried. This flavour can be leached out to other foods in slow cooking processes. But when it comes to salad making, there are no such processes and the herbs used here should, where possible, be fresh, ready and eager to give their flavour and bouquet to the ingredients they associate with. The best salad herbs are extremely delicate and, once dried, taste and smell like slightly mouldy dried grass rather than their true selves.

You only need a window ledge to grow most herbs. Keep the basil inside and the rest outside (see list below). A few fresh herbs will bring individuality and distinction to the most mundane salad.

To flavour salads with dried herbs, beat them well into the dressing shortly before you pour it over the salad. Never sprinkle them across the top of a completed salad since they cannot transmit their flavour to the salad by just sitting there, and, in fact, are more likely to stick in your throat.

Basil Basileus is the Greek word for king. Basil is the holy *tulsi* of the Hindus. If you are going to grow just one herb this should be it. Germinate the seeds in a warm space in mid-spring, pot them up and grow indoors on a south-facing window sill. Established basil plants can also sometimes be bought from nurserymen and some good Italian delicatessens in late spring and early summer. We have had great success growing the plants outdoors under continuous polythene cloches. The large-leaved sweet basil is much superior to the peppery, tiny-leaved bush basil but the latter is slightly hardier and sprigs of its leaves make an interesting addition to green salads. At the end of the growing season basil leaves can be preserved under good olive oil.

The sweet fragrant flavour of basil is superb with tomatoes and sweet peppers. Its fragrance is soon lost and it is best added to salads just before serving. Basil leaves should be torn not chopped.

Chervil   A small, delicate, feathery-leaved plant best grown in light shade to deter the plants from running to seed. Sow outdoors in succession from early spring onwards.

Chervil has a mild aniseed flavour and is excellent in cream dressings, with eggs and is a constituent with parsley, chives and tarragon in the traditional French mixture, *fines herbes*. Like basil its flavour is soon lost and it is best added to the dressing or salad just prior to serving.

Chives   Buy the plants in spring. If they are to be kept in a pot they must be kept well fed and watered. Keep several plants and keep them well trimmed back with scissors.

Chives, like chervil, go well with all dairy products. They have a delicate flavour and though they look attractive on a potato salad they really have not got the guts to liven up bland potatoes on their own. Their pretty blue flowers can look very decorative.

Coriander   Fresh green coriander is very popular in the Middle East and is readily obtainable in this country from Indian and Middle-Eastern stores. Coriander is quite easy to grow, but the home-grown herb is never as good as that which reaches us from Cyprus for most of the year.

Coriander leaf has an odour of cats, nothing so aptly describes it. This smell gives no clue to the excellent flavour which brings a subtle taste to many dishes.

Dill   A favourite herb throughout much of northern Europe. Buckets and buckets of dill can be seen in flower-like bouquets in markets in Copenhagen and Stockholm. It is surprising it is so seldom seen in this country.

Dill can be easily grown. Sow in succession from early spring onwards as it rapidly runs to seed. We think it is a herb well worth cultivating, though it will not grow properly in pots.

Try dill with potatoes, cucumbers, cream, tomato soups and oily fish. Dried dill does retain much of the herb's natural flavour but of course it entirely lacks the visual appeal of the delicate feathery fresh leaf.

Fennel   An extremely attractive plant from early spring through till autumn and well worth growing for its appearance alone. It is easy to grow in any reasonably sunny position. In mild districts new growth appears immediately the old has died back, and a mature plant will grow over two metres high. Fennel can be grown in pots, but it will not thrive.

All parts of the plant have culinary uses. Chop the abundant, aniseed-flavoured leaves and use freely with grated carrot and more sparingly over cauliflower, cucumber, green beans and salad potatoes. Branches of young fennel leaves make particularly attractive garnishes as they have a high resistance to wilting.

Hyssop   Another attractive, easy-to-grow herb which will thrive in pots, this evergreen perennial can grow to a height of half a metre.

Hyssop is just the herb to make a green leaf salad out of the ordinary. Its flavour is bitter, predominantly of mint but with many subtle underflavours. Take care, this flavour is strong. Choose only the young, tender leaves and use them sparingly, or for a more delicate flavour use just the tiny, bright blue flowers.

Marjoram   This has a mild, pleasant flavour. It is half hardy and grows to about 30 cm (12 in). You can keep a winter supply by potting plants in late summer and keeping them indoors.

Mint   There are innumerable varieties of mint. The two best readily available for culinary uses are the common spearmint and the round-leaved Apple- or Bowles-mint, though the less-common Moroccan mint is best of all. If you only wish to grow one type, it is safer to grow the Apple-mint as it is resistant to rust disease which is frequently fatal to the spearmint variety. Mint grows very easily in damp, sunny or semi-shaded positions. It is a good idea to confine the plants in sunken, bottomless buckets to prevent the underground runners from strangling less robust plants.

Mint is used extensively in Middle-Eastern cooking and it appears in a number of recipes in this book.

Oregano or wild marjoram　To our knowledge, oregano is the only herb that is better dried than fresh. Oregano bought abroad in southern Italy, Greece, Provence or Spain has far more fragrance than that generally available in this country. Look out for it when you are on holiday or ask a friend to bring you some back but be warned that customs officials can show an unusual interest in such fragrant-smelling green substances.

Use oregano as an alternative to fresh basil. In southern Italy the two are often used together over tomato salads.

Parsley　The only problem with growing parsley is that the seeds sometimes take a time to germinate. A continuous supply of this herb can be arranged by covering parsley growing in open ground with cloches or by bringing pot-grown parsley indoors to a light position. Flat-leaved or continental parsley, as it is called in the shops, has more flavour than the curly-leaved varieties. Look out for big bunches of this flat-leaved type in your Greek or Indian food shops, particularly in winter and spring when your local green-grocer or supermarket may have ceased to stock the herb.

When parsley is plentiful and cheap use it lavishly. Far too often, people thoughtlessly scatter it in tiny amounts over every dish. It is far better to consider carefully which dishes it best complements and to use it heavily on those alone. Dried parsley detracts from any dish it is added to.

Tarragon　French tarragon should sue the common Russian tarragon for defamation of character. It is quite a different plant and growing the Russian variety is a waste of time and space. French tarragon seldom sets seeds and therefore packets of seeds marked tarragon are invariably the worthless Russian type. You will have to buy plants of French tarragon. It is a semi-hardy perennial that will need some protection in severe weather. It dies right back to the ground in late autumn. To keep healthy plants it is necessary to re-propagate every second or third year by careful division of the root stocks or, better still, by tip cuttings. Tarragon does best in a sunny position in moist rich soil. It will grow in pots if they are large enough. Although it is one of the 'grande' culinary herbs its use in salads is usually confined to flavouring green salads, or in conjunction with chervil, parsley and chives in *fines herbes* dressings. It has a great affinity with fish and chicken dishes and is delicious in mayonnaise.

Thyme   Not really a salad herb but such a cheerful little plant that grows so easily on a window ledge or in a barren little patch of earth that it would be a pity not to encourage it.

Thyme is probably the most extensively used culinary herb. Fresh thyme is wonderful and thyme plucked in young flower and dried and kept on its little branches seems to keep its sweet fragrance, but dried thyme in bottles or packets brings a musty, acrid taste to any casserole to which it is added.

Spices

Try to buy and keep all spices in their natural state, that is as pods and seeds. Few packages and wrappings will protect the potency of the spice as well as Nature does – vacuum packing is fine until you have to break the seal; seldom do you use all the ground spice immediately and ground spices rapidly lose their flavour.

You will, of course, need a mortar and pestle (or a coffee grinder) to grind the pods and seeds to powder. If you do need to use ground spices buy them in small quantities. Many Indian shops sell spices very cheaply; their regular customers demand good quality and ensure a rapid turnover. It is better and cheaper to buy your spices from these shops and replace old stock with new at regular intervals than to pay the earth for presentation jars and packets in super-markets, delicatessens, or fancy herbalists. Keep spices out of the light in airtight jars. Many seeds are best lightly dry roasted or toasted in a heavy, cast-iron pan prior to grinding. This really brings out the flavour, especially with cumin and coriander seeds.

Caraway These seeds are small, dark, curved and pungent. They are used extensively in Austrian and Hungarian cooking, fre-quently in association with paprika. The flavour is very strong and not everyone's favourite. Use caraway seeds with discretion in cabbage salads.

Coriander This spice can be grown for its seeds in this country but since they are very cheap to buy, it is seldom worth the effort to cultivate them. If you do grow coriander, the seeds must not be picked until they are fully ripe, or else their flavour is unpleasant.

The small, ball-like seeds crush easily and have a mild, sweet, citrus flavour. Coriander combines well with lemon flavours and is used in almost all the world's cuisines.

Cumin A common seasoning in Mexican and Middle-Eastern cooking. Its seeds visually resemble caraway but are paler, less curved, and their flavour is quite different. Indeed cumin freshly toasted and ground is one of the finest smells ever to come from a kitchen.

Ground cumin does wonders for bean salads. It is also very good with low-fat dairy products such as yoghurt and cottage cheese and is a major constituent in those delicious Middle-Eastern nut and spice dressings.

Juniper The small blue-black berries have much more flavour than the reddish-brown ones. They should be crushed before use. Juniper brings a pleasant flavour to red cabbage salads.

Mustard If you use powdered English mustard you must add cold water to it and let it stand for at least 10 minutes to let the characteristic flavour develop. If you do not or you add hot water or vinegar you will get a milder, bitter taste which we do not like but which agrees with some people.

We generally prefer to use the slightly softer Dijon or the milder Wiltshire mustards to give bite to vinaigrette or cream dressings. You can achieve quite a different sweet flavour from mustard seeds by popping them in a small quantity of very hot oil in a small saucepan. Pour the mustard seeds and oil out of the hot saucepan immediately the seeds have popped or else they will carbonize and spoil. The seeds and flavoured oil are very good over carrots and other young vegetables.

Pepper When we say 'season with pepper', we invariably mean freshly ground black pepper. Occasionally, we will use freshly ground white pepper when, in, say, a mayonnaise, we may not want black flecks to show in a pale sauce. We may use *cayenne pepper*, which is powdered hot red chillies, for the same purpose, but when we need a hotter, less aromatic taste. *Paprika pepper*, derived from ripe red capsicums or bell peppers which are dried and ground, is mild and sweet and goes well with many vegetables and dairy products. We find that the best paprika is bright red not orange. It is worthwhile noting and sticking to a good supply as many paprikas have a harsh, sawdust-like taste. Hungarian paprika, particularly that sold in small silver packets, seems to be the most reliable.

Other flavourings

Fresh root ginger This is very reasonably priced and is obtainable in most Middle-Eastern, Chinese and Indian shops. Try to select smooth-skinned young rhizomes. Peel and hand-grate the ginger and mix the shreds with chopped spring onions, shallots, chillies, shoyu sauce or sesame oil and use over beansprouts, cucumber or tender young vegetables.

Hot pepper sauce Hot pepper sauce is a useful alternative to fresh chillies. It has a smoother taste than cayenne pepper and it is easier to adjust the heat of a dressing with it than with the powdered chilli. Hot pepper sauce comes in many styles with all sorts of additions but we find the simple Singapore-style sauce complete with seeds and available from most Chinese grocers is the best.

Shoyu sauce (soy sauce) We think the natural shoyu sauce, generally Japanese in origin and obtainable from whole- and health-food shops, is greatly superior to the soy sauce on sale in supermarkets and Chinese produce merchants. Natural shoyu has a rounder, fuller, more mellow flavour than ordinary soy sauce which is chemically produced and often has a harsh, slightly metallic taste. We use the paler varieties of shoyu as they do not spoil the colours of bright salad vegetables.

Tahini (sesame paste) This thick, peanut-butter-like paste made from crushed sesame seeds is a delicious and nutritious flavouring. Thin it down with water, yoghurt and lemon juice and add other flavours to make many tasty dips and dressings.

NOTE:
UNLESS OTHERWISE SPECIFIED,
ALL THE RECIPES IN THIS BOOK
ARE FOR 4 PEOPLE.

SPRING SALADS

Spring is not the easiest season in which to find a wide variety of good salad ingredients, so now is the time to exercise most discrimination and to make full use of the store cupboard. Winter vegetables that have been put away by the farmers and wholesalers are getting a little tired, fruit is losing its crispness and the local farmer is mainly sowing and planting rather than harvesting. All is not lost, however, since spring starts earlier in sunnier latitudes and we can rely on imported produce to add variety to the home-grown fruit and vegetables. Again, care is needed in buying since some produce travels better than others and some fruits and vegetables can be very costly.

Recommended fruit and vegetables

The vegetables at their best at this time and the ones we most recommend for spring salads are radishes, new potatoes, little white turnips, asparagus, watercress and indoor-grown spinach. Also make good use of mushrooms and beansprouts. Worthwhile imports are courgettes, mangetout peas, green beans, tomatoes, chicory, calabrese, curly endive, cucumbers and red and yellow peppers. Parsley and particularly mint are the readily available fresh herbs and these are useful for garnishes and dressings. Of the fruits available, all citrus fruits, plus pineapples, bananas and avocados are the best buys.

Radishes served with aperitifs or as a starter

This recipe is the simplest one in the book, and that is its virtue. The bright red roots and fresh green leaves of the radishes are arranged on a plain white plate or cascading over ice cubes in a glass bowl set on a sparkling white tablecloth. Any good-quality radishes can be used, but the variety French Breakfast, with their white tips, look best of all when served in this way.

3–4 radishes per person

Buy the very best-looking radishes you can find. Wash them well, putting aside any that are marked or misshapen. Now cut off the tap root only and remove the first two leaves (the seedling leaves). Place the radishes in the fridge and leave them for at least one hour before serving.

The clean, crisp, slightly peppery taste of the radishes makes them excellent partners to nearly all the traditional aperitifs or cocktails.

Alternatively, serve the radishes with fresh brown bread, butter and sea salt as a very simple but effective first course.

Minted New Potatoes with Parsley Vinaigrette

Around the time the first shoots of mint are braving the spring weather, the availability of little brown, pebble-like new potatoes is much improved. They can be found from Christmas onwards, though the earlier you buy them the more they will cost. These very small potatoes have a wonderful earthy taste which we like to complement with a simple tangy dressing.

700–900 g (1½–2 lb) small new potatoes
salt to taste
2–3 sprigs fresh mint
150 ml (5 fl oz) Vinaigrette Dressing (page 152)
15 ml (1 heaped tablespoon) fresh finely chopped parsley

Wash the potatoes clean under a running tap. Do not scrub or peel them, just cut out any damaged areas. Drop them into a pan of boiling salted water, add the mint, and cook on medium heat for 20 minutes or more. Sometimes these potatoes are very dense and take a surprisingly long time to cook. Test new potatoes by lifting one of the larger ones out with a wooden spoon and giving it a gentle squeeze. If it 'gives' a little it's cooked. Drain potatoes and set aside in a serving bowl to cool.

Mix together the vinaigrette and parsley then pour over the cooled potatoes.

New Potatoes with Spinach in Lemon-Flavoured Yoghurt Dressing

Potatoes and spinach make splendid bedfellows. The stringent, slightly bitter taste of the spinach gives the rather dour-tasting potatoes a necessary lift.

If you have bought spinach for another meal, select the smaller, fresher leaves for this salad. Use slightly large new potatoes rather than the very small ones.

700 g (1½ lb) new potatoes
12 spinach leaves, shredded
½ bunch spring onions, chopped
juice of ½ a lemon
150 ml (5 oz) natural yoghurt
salt and black pepper to taste

Cook the potatoes as described in the recipe above and allow them to cool. Set aside a small amount of shredded spinach leaves and spring onions for garnishing, then combine the remaining ingredients with the potatoes in a serving bowl. Mix well, garnish with reserved spinach and spring onions and serve.

Tomatoes in Hot Green Tomato Sauce

At the beginning and end of the local tomato-growing season there are lots of green and part-green (backward) tomatoes available. They often go to waste because we have been conditioned to eat tomatoes only when they are red. This is a shame as the hard backward fruit usually has the best flavour. With this recipe you get the best of both worlds.

6 medium-sized, ripe tomatoes
2 spring onions, complete with green leaves
1 medium green or partially green tomato
15 ml (1 tablespoon) fresh coarsely chopped parsley
15 ml (1 tablespoon) cottage cheese
1 clove garlic
¼ small fresh or dried red chilli pepper or
1.25 ml (¼ teaspoon) chilli sauce
salt and black pepper to taste

Quarter the ripe tomatoes and set them aside. Make the dressing. Wash and trim the spring onions, removing any damaged leaves. Chop them roughly and place them in a liquidizer or food processor. Quarter the green tomato and add that and the remaining ingredients to the liquidizer.

Pulse for a few seconds at high speed. Test and adjust the seasoning. Pour the dressing over the reserved quartered tomatoes, mix well.

Asparagus with Eggs Mollet

Asparagus is one of the delights of the year and although it may be expensive you don't have to have fillet steak to accompany it. Nor does it have to be just a starter to a multi-course meal. For a feast that won't cost you a fortune, accompany this recipe with Minted New Potatoes (page 42) or some good wholemeal bread and a plain green salad of crisp chilled Cos lettuce leaves.

450–900 g (1–2 lb) asparagus
(amount depends on your purse)
4 eggs (free range if possible)
sea salt to taste

Prepare the asparagus as described on page 13 and put it on to cook. It will take an average of 10 minutes but a lot will depend on your cooking method and on the thickness of the stalks. To be sure of not overcooking it, stand guard over the pan.

Five or six minutes before you think the asparagus will be cooked (eggs mollet are halfway between soft-boiled and hard-boiled), gently lower the eggs into medium-boiling water. Now gather your friends or family around your dining table and serve the asparagus on one large warm plate immediately it is cooked. Place the eggs in egg cups alongside the spears. Don't bother to peel the eggs but just cut off the tops. Each person simply dips their asparagus into the eggs and then seasons it with salt, as required.

Courgettes in Olive Oil and Lemon Dressing

This side salad is best served warm and the dressing poured on at the last moment. Broccoli can be prepared in the same manner.

The aromatic oil gives off an evocative scent of summer climes as it
is poured over the warm vegetables.

30–45 ml (2–3 tablespoons) olive oil
juice of ½ a lemon
2.5 ml (½ teaspoon) brown sugar
salt and black pepper to taste
450–700 g (1–1½ lb) small courgettes

Combine the olive oil, lemon juice, sugar and seasoning to taste.
Mix well and set aside.

Cook the courgettes whole in a pan of rapidly boiling water for
8–10 minutes. Test one for readiness by giving it a gentle squeeze
– if it 'gives' a little, it is cooked. Drain and cool the courgettes
briefly under running cold water. (This enables you to handle the
courgettes more easily, and it also helps keep the skins bright
green.)

Top and tail the courgettes and cut them up into 1 cm (½ in)
rounds. Place them in a serving bowl. Pour over the dressing, mix
well, check the seasoning and serve immediately.

Baby Turnips in Horseradish
Cream Sauce

Turnips are the first of the locally grown outdoor crops to be ready
for eating. Use only small firm turnips for salads. Reject any roots
that are soft and spongy. This is a simple salad but a first-rate one to
accompany cold pork or beef or it could be served as part of a
selection of salads.

1 bunch [about 450 g (1 lb)] fresh young white turnips
30 ml (2 tablespoons) horseradish sauce
30 ml (2 tablespoons) whipping cream
lemon juice to taste
salt and black pepper to taste

Peel and grate the turnips. If they are soggy, toss them in a clean cloth and squeeze out excess moisture. Put the turnips into a serving bowl and stir in the other ingredients. Test for seasoning and serve.

Chicory, Avocado and Watercress Salad in Orange Vinaigrette

The mildly bitter taste of the chicory contrasts well with the slight sweetness of both the avocado and the orange dressing, and the greens of the salad and the colour of the garnishing are very appetizing.

1 small avocado, peeled and chopped
½ bunch watercress, discoloured leaves discarded, shredded
3 heads of prepared chicory, cut into 2-cm (¾-in) slices
30 ml (2 tablespoons) Vinaigrette Dressing (page 152)
30 ml (2 tablespoons) fresh orange juice
salt and black pepper to taste
orange slices to garnish

Combine the avocado, watercress and chicory in a salad bowl. Mix together the vinaigrette and orange juice and pour it over the salad. Season to taste. Toss the salad gently and serve garnished with four orange slices.

Cauliflower Salad

For this salad the cauliflower is parboiled and should remain firm and still crisp. It is tossed in a hot dressing before chilling to ensure the cauliflower absorbs the full flavour of the dressing. The finished salad is garnished with chopped anchovies or olives before serving.

1 small cauliflower, cleaned
salt
60 ml (4 tablespoons) olive oil
30 ml (2 tablespoons) lemon juice
1 clove garlic, crushed
pinch of cayenne
2.5 ml (½ teaspoon) French mustard
black pepper to taste
4 tinned anchovies, chopped or 7 or 8 black olives

Choose a pan big enough to take the whole cauliflower. Add 2.5 cm (1 in) salted water. Cover and boil the cauliflower for 6 to 7 minutes. Drain it and run it under cold water until it is cool enough to handle. Cut the cauliflower into small florets and put them into a serving bowl.

Combine the oil, lemon juice, garlic, cayenne, mustard and seasoning to taste in a small pan and bring the mixture to the boil. Whisk it well together and pour it over the cauliflower. Toss well and set the salad in the refrigerator to chill. Just before serving, garnish the top with chopped anchovies or black olives.

VARIATIONS

● Replace half the cauliflower with a head of green broccoli.

● Try the parboiled cauliflower with Green Vinaigrette Dressing (page 153) with the addition of two cloves of garlic.

• Try the cauliflower or the cauliflower/broccoli combination with Strong Blue Cheese Dressing (page 169).

Coriander Cream Eggs

We've given two versions of this recipe. The first is colourful and elegant and makes egg mayonnaise look like a country bumpkin! The second version makes a cheerful, wholesome, filling bowl salad.

150 ml (5 oz) Coriander Cream Sauce (page 168)
4 hardboiled eggs, quartered
100 g (4 oz) white button mushrooms, stalks trimmed off
juice of ½ a lemon
about 20 black olives
4 sprigs of coriander to garnish

Take 4 plain white side plates. Place a good 15 ml (heaped tablespoon) of the green coriander sauce in the centre of each. Arrange the quartered eggs, yellow side up, around this.

Finely slice the mushrooms and place them around the eggs. Dress the mushroom slices with lemon juice. Scatter the black olives over the plates and garnish the completed salad with the coriander sprigs.

VARIATION
300 ml (12 fl oz) Coriander Cream Sauce (page 168)
300 ml (12 oz) cooked macaroni or pasta shells
100 g (4 oz) white button mushrooms, quartered
juice of 1 small lemon
about 20 black olives
4 hardboiled eggs, quartered
roughly chopped coriander leaves to garnish

Place the sauce, macaroni, mushrooms and lemon juice in a bowl and mix well. Gently fold in the eggs and the olives. Turn into a serving bowl and garnish with the chopped coriander leaves.

Strawberry and Cucumber Salad

This cheerful, light, formal salad brings with it the promise of better days to come. The first strawberries always make a special impact and when used like this, a few go far. Often those first Mediterranean fruits are quite tart and are better treated this way than served as a dessert. Lime juice has just the correct balance of sweetness and acidity to enhance both the main ingredients.

A fine side salad to accompany poached mackerel or cold cooked poultry.

half a cucumber (about 225 g/8 oz)
salt and black pepper to taste
175 g (6 oz) strawberries, washed, drained and hulled
juice of ½ a lime

Peel the cucumber and slice it wafer-thin. Spread these slices in concentric circles over 4 individual plates. Lightly dust the cucumber with salt and black pepper. Quarter the strawberries and pile them in the centre of each plate. Dress with the lime juice and chill before serving.

Minted Chicory Salad

Chicory is a very useful salad vegetable so long as its slight bitterness is carefully complemented by the other ingredients. In this salad we cover a gamut of flavours ranging from the bitterness of the chicory to the sweetness of the orange.

½ small head lettuce, shredded
½ medium Spanish onion, finely sliced
2 heads prepared chicory, cut into 2-cm (¾-in) slices
1 sweet orange, peeled, sliced and chopped
30 ml (2 tablespoons) fresh mint, chopped
30 ml (2 tablespoons) Vinaigrette Dressing (page 152)

Layer the lettuce in the bottom of a salad bowl. Combine the other ingredients in a mixing bowl and toss them well together. Mound this salad on top of the lettuce leaves and serve.

Mangetout and Avocado Salad

SERVES 4 TO 6

If the mangetout are very young and tender just top and tail them and use them raw in the salad. If a little older, boil them very briefly as directed in the recipe. Mangetout deteriorate very quickly, so buy only the freshest, flat pods (any pods in which the peas have been allowed to develop will already be stringy and starchy). Finally, if in doubt, don't buy them, they're expensive.

450 g (1 lb) mangetout peas (top and tail and remove strings,
if necessary)
2 small–medium avocados, peeled and chopped small
50 g (2 oz) small fresh mushrooms, finely sliced
30 ml (2 tablespoons) olive oil
15 ml (1 tablespoon) lemon juice
salt and black pepper
30 ml (2 tablespoons) parsley, finely chopped, to garnish

Either use raw mangetout or drop them into a pan of boiling water and boil for 2–3 minutes, drain them and rinse under cold water. Combine the peas, avocados, mushrooms, olive oil, lemon

juice, salt and black pepper and toss them well together. Garnish
with parsley and serve.

Leeks with Soured Cream Dressing

For this recipe the little finger-thick leeks available in late spring-
time are a delight. Unfortunately, while plentiful on the conti-
nent, this 'poor man's asparagus' is difficult to obtain in Britain.
There is no real reason for this as we grow plenty of leeks on to full
size. If you live in the country you may have more success than
town folk in finding the young vegetables. When they are obtainable they are very reasonably priced and well worth pursuing.

700 g (1½ lb) prepared leeks
salt to taste
75 ml (3 fl oz) Mayonnaise (page 154)
75 ml (3 fl oz) soured cream
2 or 3 spring onions, finely chopped
30 ml (2 tablespoons) finely chopped parsley
black pepper

Place the leeks horizontally in a pan of rapidly boiling salted water
sufficient to just cover them. Cook for 6–8 minutes or until a table
fork can pierce the white flesh. Cool immediately under cold
running water. Drain.

Combine the mayonnaise, soured cream and spring onions.
Arrange the leeks in a shallow serving dish and pour over the
dressing. Garnish with parsley, add freshly ground black pepper to
taste, and serve.

VARIATION

For a thinner sauce and slightly sharper taste, replace the mayonnaise with the same amount of Vinaigrette Dressing (page 152).

Broccoli with Lemon Egg Mayonnaise

Use purple or white broccoli but choose the youngest, most tender shoots.

450 g (1 lb) broccoli separated into florets, stalks cut to about
8 cm (3 in) in length
15 ml (1 tablespoon) lemon juice
2 hardboiled eggs, finely chopped
100 ml (4 fl oz) Mayonnaise (page 154)

Place the broccoli in a pan of rapidly boiling salted water sufficient to just cover. Cook for 6–8 minutes. Drain, cool under cold running water and drain again. Whisk the lemon juice and chopped egg into the mayonnaise and pour over the broccoli. Serve.

VARIATION
Serve the broccoli lukewarm dressed simply with a lemon-flavoured vinaigrette.

Avocado and Pink Grapefruit Salad

A salad of simple contrasts, soft green set against soft pink. The almost excessive richness of the avocado is cut here by the sharpness of the grapefruit which in its turn is made to taste sweet by having dribbled over it at the last moment a small quantity of even sharper vinegar.

4 medium Hass avocados, peeled and sliced
salt and freshly ground black pepper
2 pink grapefruit, peeled, with all traces of pith removed
60 ml (4 tablespoons) oil
20 ml (4 teaspoons) wine or cider vinegar

Arrange the slices of avocado radial fashion on 4 small plain plates. Season well with the salt and black pepper.

Separate the grapefruit into segments and cut each segment in half. Pile these half-segments in the centre of each plate. Dress the salad with oil and just before serving sprinkle the grapefruit with the vinegar.

Cucumber with Sesame Ginger Dressing

This nutty dip is good with any vegetable crudités, but it is especially good with cucumber. The sweet sesame oil is an important constituent of this dressing so it is best not to substitute.

30 ml (2 tablespoons) tahini

30 ml (2 tablespoons) natural yoghurt or water

15 ml (1 tablespoon) sesame oil

5 ml (1 teaspoon) vinegar

5 ml (1 teaspoon) shoyu or soy sauce

1 clove garlic, crushed

1 almond-sized piece of fresh ginger, peeled and crushed

dash of hot pepper sauce

black pepper to taste

½ large cucumber

5 ml (1 teaspoon) sesame seeds to garnish

Combine all the ingredients except the cucumber and sesame seeds in a small bowl. Mix well together and pile the mixture in the centre of a large serving plate.

Cut the cucumber down the middle and remove the seeds with the back of a teaspoon. Cut the cucumber into strips 8 cm (3 in) long and arrange these in and around the mound of dressing like the spokes of a wheel. Sprinkle with sesame seeds.

VARIATION

Use 350 g (12 oz) beansprouts instead of the cucumber. Stir the shoots well into the dressing and then sprinkle with the sesame seeds.

Coriander Mushrooms

This elegant salad has become something of a modern classic. It is simple to prepare, but do please note the following points. The rich aromatic flavour of olive oil is essential to this salad, so don't substitute any other. We have had the mushrooms served to us awash in a weak-flavoured juice: avoid this by cooking the mushrooms, uncovered, in a small frying pan or sauté pan (not a high-sided saucepan). Preferably, use small button mushrooms, but failing these, large ones, halved or quartered, will do fine. Whichever type you choose, they must be very fresh.

60 ml (4 tablespoons) olive oil
5 ml (1 teaspoon) coriander seeds, freshly ground
1 bay leaf
250 g (9 oz) white button mushrooms, stems trimmed
10 ml (2 teaspoons) lemon juice
salt and pepper to taste
bay leaves and lemon portions to garnish

Heat the olive oil in a sauté pan over medium heat. Add the ground coriander and the bay leaf to the hot oil. Immediately the bay leaf starts to darken, tip in the mushrooms and add the lemon juice.

Season with salt and pepper and cook, stirring frequently, for 3–4 minutes or until the mushrooms have a translucent look about them (achieved when the hot oil has penetrated the centre). Adjust seasoning, allow to cool, place in serving dish or dishes, and chill. Garnish with bay leaves and lemon sections before serving.

Cucumber and Thick Yoghurt Dressing

Cucumber and yoghurt are a winning combination. Flavoured with garlic, mint and cumin they appear throughout the Middle East in many forms under such names as *raita*, *cacik*, *tzatziki* or *jajig*. This deluxe version is closest to the Greek *tzatziki*. If you haven't the time to drain the yoghurt or deseed the cucumber don't worry, it will still taste good, but it is then best eaten as soon as it is prepared.

salt
½ cucumber, deseeded and finely chopped
275 ml (10 fl oz) Strained Natural Yoghurt (page 159)
1 clove garlic, crushed
8 fresh mint leaves, finely chopped
1.25 ml (¼ teaspoon) dry-roasted and ground cumin seed, optional
sprigs of mint to garnish

Scatter the salt over the cucumber and place it in a colander to drain for 30 minutes. Lightly press out any excess moisture and place the cucumber in a mixing bowl. Stir in the remaining ingredients, check for seasoning and transfer to a serving dish. Garnish with sprigs of mint.

Green Beans and Sweetcorn with Tomato Mayonnaise

A pretty, mild-flavoured salad as welcome in spring, made from imported beans and tinned sweetcorn, as it is in late summer, made with fresh, home-grown vegetables.

225 g (8 oz) French beans

150 g (3 oz) tin sweetcorn kernels (or 1 large head of corn,
cooked and scraped)

2 ripe tomatoes

150 ml (5 fl oz) Mayonnaise (page 154)

salt and black pepper to taste

Top and tail the beans and drop them into a saucepan of rapidly boiling salted water for 4–6 minutes, until cooked but still retaining a little bite. Drain and cool immediately under cold running water. Cut the cooked French beans into 5-cm (2-in) lengths and set them aside.

Cut the tomatoes in half and shake out the seeds and the excess juice. Chop the flesh up finely and put it into a small mixing bowl. Pour in the mayonnaise and with a fork beat together until the mayonnaise is well coloured. Add the green beans and corn, season with salt and pepper, mix well and serve.

Spinach and Walnut Salad with Mint and Lemon Dressing

Tender young spinach leaves available in the late spring can be used to make a green salad. These small, fleshy leaves have a surprisingly mild flavour and are of course most nutritious. The toasted walnuts in the recipe give the salad an unexpected crunch.

100 g (4 oz) young spinach leaves, discard any damaged or
discoloured leaves
2–3 spring onions, chopped
30 ml (2 tablespoons) chopped walnuts, lightly toasted
30 ml (2 tablespoons) olive oil
15 ml (1 tablespoon) lemon juice
15 ml (1 tablespoon) fresh mint, finely chopped
salt and black pepper to taste

Wash the spinach leaves individually and carefully, cut off the
stems and chop the leaves into very thin shreds. Mix them with the
spring onions and walnuts. Combine the olive oil, lemon juice,
mint and salt and black pepper to taste and mix well. Toss the salad
in this dressing and serve.

Avocado and Yoghurt Salad

Prepare this salad with firm but not underripe avocado pears.
Smooth-skinned avocados should give just a little if gently
squeezed between finger and thumb, but they will be quite soft
around the neck. The alligator-skinned Hass avocados can be
softer, but don't buy them if the skin has begun to shrink.

2 medium-sized avocado pears
225 ml (8 fl oz) natural yoghurt
1 clove garlic, finely chopped
15 ml (1 tablespoon) fresh walnuts
salt to taste
sprigs of parsley to garnish
black pepper

Peel the avocados and cut the flesh into medium-sized chunks. Put
the yoghurt in a serving bowl and stir in the garlic, walnuts and

salt to taste. Stir in the avocado chunks, garnish with sprigs of
parsley and finish the salad off with a few grindings of black
pepper.

Endive and Walnut Salad

The curly mop-headed endive available in winter and spring has a
faintly bitter flavour that sharpens the taste buds. Try this salad as a
starter or side salad.

450 g (1 lb) endive leaves
50 g (2 oz) walnuts, chopped
10 ml (2 teaspoons) French mustard
30 ml (2 tablespoons) olive oil
15 ml (1 tablespoon) wine vinegar
salt and black pepper to taste

Discard any damaged or discoloured endive leaves, trim the stems
off, wash the leaves one by one and drain them. Put the leaves in a
salad bowl with the nuts. Put the mustard in a small bowl and
slowly beat in the oil. Stir in the vinegar and salt and pepper to
taste. Pour the dressing over the salad, toss well and serve.

VARIATION

Replace the walnuts with lightly toasted pine nuts or (for non-
vegetarians) sizzling-hot lardons of bacon. Top with a handful of
hot Traditional Croûtons (page 162).

Asparagus with Sesame Seed and Soy Dressing

In this Japanese-inspired recipe the asparagus is only parcooked. If you prefer softer cooked asparagus (although it should always retain some 'bite'), increase the cooking time given by 3 to 4 minutes.

20 spears of asparagus, trimmed, cut into
4-cm (1½-in) lengths
salt
60 ml (4 tablespoons) Sesame Seed and Soy Dressing
(page 174)

Drop the asparagus into a pan of slow-boiling salted water, cook for 5 minutes and drain. Rinse immediately under cold water until the asparagus is cooled. Drain. Put the dressing in a mixing bowl, add the asparagus and toss together lightly. Divide the asparagus lengths between four small bowls and serve.

Celeriac Rémoulade

Plain looking but very tasty, celeriac rémoulade is one of the most popular constituents of the traditional vegetable *crudités* presented in countless small eating places in France. The recipe does not demand great exactness; the celeriac, mustard, mayonnaise and vinegar are happy companions. Soften the taste with cream if you like.

1 large celeriac root [about 450 g (16 oz)]
lemon juice or vinegar
150 ml (5 oz) Mayonnaise (page 154)
15 ml (1 tablespoon) French mustard

10 ml (2 teaspoons) white wine vinegar or lemon juice
salt and pepper to taste
50 ml (1 fl oz) thick cream (optional)

Peel the celeriac root, cutting away any brown patches. Finely slice or shred the root into long matchsticks. Put these directly into a bowl of cold water acidulated with lemon juice or vinegar. When all the celeriac is prepared, blanch it by dropping it into a pan of boiling water for no more than a minute. Drain well and mix with the rest of the ingredients. Set the salad aside in a cool place to let the flavours intermingle for at least two hours.

Spiced Potato Salad with Fresh Coriander Leaves

A hot, spicy salad that keeps well and even tastes better the day after preparation.

700 g (1½ lb) potatoes, peeled and cut into chunks – or use
small, new, whole potatoes, washed
30 ml (2 tablespoons) sesame seed oil or other vegetable oil
50 g (2 oz) sesame seeds
15 ml (1 tablespoon) mustard seeds
2.5 cm (1 in) fresh root ginger, peeled and finely grated
2.5 ml (½ teaspoon) chilli powder or hot pepper sauce
salt to taste
juice of ½ a lemon
30 ml (2 tablespoons) fresh coriander leaves, chopped

Put the potatoes in a pan with plenty of boiling water and boil them until only just tender. Remove from the heat, drain and put into a salad bowl.

Heat the oil in a frying pan and stir in the sesame seeds, mustard seeds, ginger, chilli and salt to taste. Stir-fry over a moderate heat for 3–4 minutes. Stir the oil and spices into the potatoes, add the lemon juice and mix well. Allow to cool completely.

Gently stir in the coriander leaves. Serve or chill for later use.

Radish and Cabbage Salad with Chilli Dressing

A Chinese-inspired cold salad with flavourings like chilli and sesame.

450 g (1 lb) white cabbage, finely shredded
1 bunch radish, topped, tailed and thinly sliced
salt
45 ml (3 tablespoons) sesame seed oil or other vegetable oil
½ fresh or dried chilli pepper, seeds removed, finely chopped
10 ml (2 teaspoons) freshly ground coriander seeds
15 ml (1 tablespoon) coarsely chopped coriander leaves,
optional

Combine the cabbage and radish and salt to taste. Heat the oil in a small pan and stir in the chilli and coriander. Cook and stir for 2 minutes and then stir the spiced oil into the cabbage and radish. Sprinkle with coriander leaves, if available, and serve.

VARIATION

In Chinese cookery the cabbage and radish mixture would be liberally sprinkled with salt and set aside for 3–5 hours. The mixture is then rinsed and pressed before being mixed with spiced oil.

Watercress and Radish Salad

A rather delicate-looking, but nevertheless strongly flavoured, salad. Use the freshest watercress and the crunchiest radishes you can find.

1 bunch watercress, discard yellow leaves, trim the stems, wash and drain

1 bunch radish, trimmed, washed, drained and chilled for 1 hour or more

½ small head of lettuce, washed and drained (use hearts of Webb lettuce or small Cos lettuce)

Vinaigrette Dressing (page 152)

Make a bed of lettuce leaves in rosette fashion in a serving bowl and sprinkle over a little dressing. Thinly slice the radishes and combine them with the watercress. Add vinaigrette dressing to taste and toss the mixture in it. Arrange the dressed radish and watercress on the lettuce leaves and serve.

Spinach, Mushroom and Croûton Salad

A first-course salad of dark green spinach leaves and white crunchy mushrooms and croûtons.

225 g (8 oz) summer spinach

225 g (8 oz) small mushrooms

24 Croûtons (page 162)

salt and black pepper to taste

juice of ½ a lemon

90 ml (6 tablespoons) olive oil

30 ml (2 tablespoons) white wine vinegar

Wash the spinach and drain it well. Tear the leaves into large pieces, discarding the stalks. Pile the spinach into a bowl. Wipe and slice the mushrooms, then squeeze the lemon juice over them.

Put salt and pepper into a small bowl, add the olive oil and wine vinegar, whisk until blended. Scatter the mushrooms and croûtons over the spinach, pour the dressing over, toss thoroughly and serve.

SUMMER SALADS

During the summer, everything is in the salad maker's favour, every week brings a new vegetable into season, every trip to the market means a new discovery. Although we may lose one or two short-season vegetables, as time passes there is a steady accumulation of produce. From mid-summer on, there is little need to buy anything imported; but that doesn't mean we have to isolate ourselves totally from the produce of warmer countries. They bring, for example, the small joys of a bunch of fresh basil, new 'wet' garlic from Provence, Italian plum tomatoes, the mild, sweet Spanish onions and, of course, vegetables like aubergines which, although now grown here commercially, are cheaper and tastier when grown in warmer climates.

With such a choice it pays to buy with discretion. Shop around, choose the freshest produce and don't buy too much, since vegetables spoil quickly in warm weather. Be careful about buying too many bargains during the summer. They have to be used immediately and you don't save much when everything else is relatively cheap. Leaf vegetables past their prime are never a bargain, and sorting through faded fruit and vegetables is always a thankless, time-consuming task. Chide your greengrocer if something is not up to scratch. Compliment him when it's particularly pleasing. Such information is useful to him when he next goes to market. At this time of the year he, too, can shop around. For quality and economy, here is a broad outline of what to look out for as the season progresses.

Early summer Imported courgettes, outdoor lettuce, broad beans, imported kidney beans, carrots, beetroot, globe artichokes, garden peas and tomatoes.

Mid-summer Courgettes, fresh garlic (French), French beans,

Italian plum tomatoes, Spanish onions, celery, cauliflower.

Late summer   Runner beans, broccoli, Italian fennel, peppers, corn on the cob, apples.

Summer herbs   A few pot-grown herbs can transform the range and tastes of summer salads. Keep basil indoors on a sunny window sill, parsley, mint, chives and tarragon in well-watered pots outside. Given just a tiny plot of land, dill, chervil and fennel will more than earn their keep. That same little plot can also be used to grow the rediscovered salad herbs, such as rocket, sorrel, lamb's lettuce and hyssop that can give interest and distinction to green salads, not just in summer, but all the year round.

Summer Green Salad

Green salads should change like the seasons. Summer green salads can be bright and colourful and good-looking enough to act as table decoration. For instance, pile a multitude of torn leaves into a big white or glass bowl and scatter the flowers of herb plants across the top. People who grow some of their own salad ingredients are often looking for ways of using them up. So decorate your table with them and not your compost heap. Even if you have to buy all your salad goods, they are cheap enough in middle and late summer for you to be carefree in their use.

Here are some thoughts on summer greens and a suggestion for a green leaf salad.

Cos and **Webb lettuce**   Long leaves and round leaves, cool and crisp.

Watercress   Spicy, peppery, dark green leaf.

Sorrel   Astringent, tangy almost lemony flavour; home-grown or picked on a walk in the park or country.

Basil   Peppery strings of tiny leaves from bush basil; grow on a sunny window ledge.

Rocket   Nutty-flavoured, rapid-growing annual, best picked young; easily home grown. Has a powerful taste, so do not use too much.

Hyssop A piquant bitterness, not to be overdone; easily grown in pot or garden.

Carefully wash summer green leaves under cold running water. Gently tear up the larger leaves. Dress and toss them just before serving with a vinaigrette of olive or walnut oil made with a low proportion of vinegar or lemon juice (4–5 parts oil to 1 part lemon).

Garnish the salad with the mild-flavoured flowers of hyssop, peppery, golden nasturtium flowers and the beautiful, blue borage.

Poor Boy Salad

SERVES 8

This salad can be found in Italian, Creole and black restaurants in New Orleans where it is cheerfully referred to as 'wop salad'. Similar salads are found in South America and the Caribbean. Serve it with grilled or roasted meats. It is wonderful with barbecued food. This salad should be made the day before it is to be eaten and will store well for days.

In New Orleans, sandwiches are called poor boys – 'Poor boy, he can only afford sandwiches'. A popular Italian version is 25 cm (10 in) round by 8 cm (3 in) high, stuffed with salad, salami, cheese and ham – some poor boy! Anyway, here is the recipe for the salad.

400 g (14 oz) tomatoes, juice and seeds removed, diced

½ a medium cucumber, diced

1 large pickled gherkin, diced

1 sweet red pepper, cored and seeded, diced

1 medium onion diced, or 4 large spring onions, including
half the green part, sliced

One or two of the following par-boiled vegetables
100 g (4 oz) of each
cauliflower, broccoli, young green beans, asparagus tips or
artichoke hearts, chopped
30 ml (2 tablespoons) capers
100 g (4 oz) green olives, pitted
½ bunch parsley, chopped
2 large cloves garlic, crushed
100 ml (4 fl oz) olive oil
30 ml (2 tablespoons) wine vinegar
10 ml (2 teaspoons) French mustard
10 ml (2 teaspoons) dried oregano
salt and black pepper to taste

Place all the ingredients in a mixing bowl. Stir well, adjust the seasoning, cover and leave to mature in a cool place for 24 hours before use.

Cos Salad in Fennel Cream Dressing

A simple variation on green salad in vinaigrette dressing which uses fresh fennel leaves. These are the delicate, feathery leaves from common fennel, one of the most imposing plants to be found in an English herb garden. You can, of course, use other fresh herbs or mixed herbs in this dressing.

10 ml (2 teaspoons) finely chopped fresh fennel leaves
225 ml (8 fl oz) single cream
10 ml (2 teaspoons) lemon juice
salt and black pepper to taste
1 medium-sized Cos lettuce, washed, dried well and
coarsely chopped

Caribbean Salad

A salad that can be made all the year round but it is cooling and refreshingly sweet on a hot summer's day. It is also good as an exotic and colourful starter for a winter meal that needs cheering up.

10 cm (4 in) piece of cucumber, quartered lengthwise and chopped crosswise
2 medium-sized just-ripe bananas, thinly sliced
2 medium-sized green peppers, seeded, cored and diced
2 sweet oranges, peeled, pith removed, separated into segments and cut into halves
150 ml (5 fl oz) natural yoghurt
15 ml (1 tablespoon) flaked almonds, lightly toasted

Combine the cucumber, bananas, green peppers and oranges in a salad bowl. Stir in the yoghurt, sprinkle almonds over the top, chill and serve.

Fresh Mint and Apple Salad

This salad is particularly refreshing on a hot summer's day and it is also a good accompaniment to hot spicy meals like curries. Try it with English apples such as George Cave or, in late summer, use Worcesters. George Cave are the first of the English apples we notice. Smallish, quite crisp, a little Cox-like in character but without the flecking, they keep quite a good white colour when cut.

3 medium eating apples, cored and diced
60 ml (4 tablespoons) chopped fresh mint
300 ml (10 fl oz) natural yoghurt
15 ml (1 tablespoon) clear honey

Combine the apples and mint in a serving bowl and pour over the yoghurt and honey. Mix well together, chill before serving.

Apple and Celery with Almond and Tahini Dressing

A light, modern version of the *maître d*'s famous creation at the Waldorf-Astoria. He was fond of saying 'my job is the serving of food, never the cooking'. Well, maybe his head chef should have said, 'I think that salad would be better done this way.'

250 g (9 oz) crisp apples, well washed
Vinaigrette Dressing (page 152)
½ head celery (250 g/9 oz) trimmed and washed
30 ml (2 tablespoons) tahini sauce
100 ml (4 fl oz) natural yoghurt
salt and pepper to taste
50 g (2 oz) flaked almonds

Core the apples and cut them into small chunks, dropping these immediately into the French dressing to prevent them from discolouring. Cut the celery sticks into 1-cm (⅜-in) sections and place them in a mixing bowl. Add the tahini and yoghurt, mix well and season to taste with salt and pepper. Thoroughly drain the apple chunks (you can use the remaining dressing another time), add them to the dressed celery and again mix well. Fold in most of the flaked almonds and turn the salad into a serving dish, decorating the top with a few reserved almonds.

Spice Street Salad

It is strange how we in the West have until recently only used heavy spicing for pickling vinegars and for smothering any unwelcome taints that may be lurking in preserved or not-so-well-preserved meats. In the Middle East spice mixtures of all different sorts are bought in little paper cones into which one dips bread or scatters over dishes just like we use salt and pepper.

Here we use one of these mixtures on the freshest of summer vegetables which have been lightly cooked and then quickly cooled to safeguard their colour and texture.

250 g (8 oz) cauliflower florets
250 g (8 oz) fresh young carrots, scrubbed, topped and tailed,
cut into thin rounds
250 g (8 oz) tender French beans, topped and tailed
30 ml (2 tablespoons) olive oil
45–60 ml (3–4 tablespoons) Spicy Almond Dressing
(page 170)

This salad is ruined if the vegetables are overcooked, so steam them together for just 3–4 minutes or cook them individually in a small amount of boiling salted water for the same length of time. Whichever cooking method you use, immediately they are cooked, plunge them under cold running water until they are quite cold.

Toss the vegetables in a mixing bowl, add the olive oil and mix well. Turn the salad onto a serving dish and sprinkle with the spicy almond dressing.

Crudités from Bio

Meals are often memorable not just for the food which was served
but also the manner in which it was presented. One such occasion
Paddy cherishes took place one lunchtime outside a small restaurant in the picturesque hill village of Bio in southern France.

The diners were a group of models (it really was a picturesque
village) and their photographers. The party of 8 were gathered
round a large, rough, wooden table. On went the white paper
tablecloths and everyone was given a fork and a small cutting
board. In quick succession the table was spread with bowls of
different dressings, a jug of thick cream, seasonings, crusty
country loaves, glasses, pitchers of chilled white wine, a large vine
rootstock hung with small salami sausages and sharp knives
dangling from small leather thongs, a plate of tiny French beans
and finally, as centrepiece and main edible attraction, a great
flower basket decoratively arranged with gleaming whole vegetables: red peppers, green peppers, tiny cauliflowers and cucumbers, quartered fennel bulbs, celery hearts, tomatoes, bouquets of
fresh herbs and a pile of lemons. Everyone was then left to compose
and dress their salads to their own liking. It kept them busy – but
not quiet – for an hour.

Dill, Pea and Potato Salad

Fresh dill goes well with potatoes, eggs, pickled fish, cream and, of
course, pickled gherkins or cucumbers. These can be combined on
a bed of lettuce hearts to make a grand salad in the Niçoise style,
but far more frequently we would use it in this simple salad.

450 g (1 lb) small potatoes, cooked
225 g (8 oz) fresh garden peas, lightly cooked
30 ml (2 tablespoons) chopped fresh dill weed

45 ml (3 tablespoons) vegetable oil
15 ml (1 tablespoon) lemon juice or white wine vinegar
5 ml (1 teaspoon) French mustard
50 ml (2 fl oz) cream, optional
salt and pepper to taste
3 or 4 dill flower heads to garnish, optional

Cut the potatoes into bite-sized pieces, turn them into a mixing bowl and add the garden peas. Beat or blend together the dill, oil, lemon juice, mustard and the cream if used. Season the dressing with salt and pepper and pour it over the potatoes and peas.

Mix together all the ingredients, turn them into a serving bowl and garnish with the dill flowers.

Courgette, Dill and Yoghurt Salad

Both the leaves and the seeds of the dill plant, a member of the parsley family, are used in cooking. The dried seeds have a more pungent flavour than the leaves which can be used fresh or dried. In this recipe we use fresh dill leaves (also called dill weed), for their milder flavour suits the yoghurt sauce better. For a special garnish use whole dill flowers or the immature seed heads. They are most attractive.

30 ml (2 tablespoons) sunflower oil or butter
700 g (1½ lb) small courgettes, topped and tailed, cut into
1-cm (½-in) rounds
10 ml (2 teaspoons) fresh dill, chopped
100 ml (4 fl oz) natural yoghurt
15 ml (1 tablespoon) lemon juice
salt and black pepper to taste
pinch of paprika

Heat the oil or butter in a pan and add the courgettes. Stir in the dill (reserving a small pinch for garnish later) and cover the pan. Cook over a moderate heat, stirring occasionally for 5–8 minutes until the courgettes are barely tender, but firm to the bite.

Transfer the contents of the pan to a bowl and allow the courgettes to cool a little. Stir in the yoghurt, lemon juice and salt and black pepper. Turn the courgettes and sauce into a serving bowl and garnish with a pinch of paprika and the reserved dill. Serve.

VARIATION
This salad can be made with dried dill when fresh is unavailable.

Courgette and Parsley Salad

A very simple but effective courgette salad. The recipe calls for dill seeds but you could use the dill seed heads retrieved from a jar of dill pickles. Incidentally, eastern European countries have a great tradition of pickling and preserving and their products are both very good and reasonably priced.

700 g (1½ lb) small courgettes
30 ml (2 tablespoons) sunflower oil or butter
60 ml (4 tablespoons) Vinaigrette Dressing (see page 152)
45 ml (3 tablespoons) fresh parsley, coarsely chopped
5 ml (1 teaspoon) dill seeds (optional)
salt and black pepper to taste

Cook the courgettes in the oil or butter, as in the previous recipe, then chill them completely under cold running water. Pat dry, then place them in a serving bowl. Add the remaining ingredients, toss them well together and serve.

Pear, Grape and Cucumber Salad

SERVES 4 TO 6

A simple, yet unusual, combination, which makes a good side salad for a dish with cheese in it or simply as an accompaniment to cheese and bread. Served well chilled, it also makes an appetizing starter. Try it with the new season Italian pears available from mid-summer onwards. Black grapes are the most impressive with this salad but they should only be used when you have time to deseed them.

Small, green, seedless grapes are available very cheaply from Spain and Cyprus in July and August.

3 ripe but firm sweet pears, peeled and cored, one pear thinly
sliced, the rest diced
½ medium cucumber, divided in half lengthwise, seeds
scooped out (slice ¼ cucumber, dice the rest)
100 g (4 oz) black or green seedless grapes, washed
Vinaigrette Dressing (see page 152)

Make a bed of the pear and cucumber slices in a small salad bowl. Put the remaining pear, cucumber and grapes (reserve 5 or 6 grapes) into a bowl and toss them in vinaigrette dressing to taste. Pour this mixture over the bed of pear and cucumber slices. Garnish the salad with the reserved grapes, chill and serve.

Simple Carrot Salad

This most simple of salads is at its best made with the sweet young English carrots available in late June, early July.

450 g (1 lb) young carrots, scrubbed and finely grated
30 ml (2 tablespoons) olive oil
15 ml (1 tablespoon) lemon juice
salt to taste

Combine all the ingredients. Toss well and serve.

VARIATION

Add a handful of chopped fresh parsley, fresh fennel or fresh chervil.

Carrot and Redcurrant Salad

The rather tart redcurrants are excellent with carrot and they make a refreshing salad with an unusual colour combination.

450 g (1 lb) carrots, scrubbed and coarsely grated
100 g (4 oz) redcurrants, removed from their stalks
15 ml (1 tablespoon) redcurrant jelly
30 ml (2 tablespoons) lemon juice

Combine the carrots and redcurrants and mix well together. Stir the redcurrant jelly into the lemon juice. Toss the salad in this mixture then set it aside in the refrigerator to chill before serving.

Gingered Carrot Salad

Grated carrot is such a good foil for so many flavours. This is a simple salad with an exotic touch.

450 g (1 lb) carrots, scrubbed and finely grated
1 walnut-sized piece of fresh ginger
1 small clove garlic, crushed
60 ml (4 tablespoons) lemon juice
salt and black pepper

Place the grated carrot in a fair-sized mixing bowl and grate the fresh ginger evenly across the surface. Beat the crushed garlic and the lemon juice together in a cup and pour it over the carrot and ginger. Season with salt and pepper and gently mix them together. Taste and adjust the seasoning, then turn the salad onto a serving dish.

Carrot and Apple Salad

Carrots and apples partner each other very well. Do not peel either the summer carrots or the apples since most of the vitamins in both are contained in the skin or just beneath it. Do, however, remember to wash both well in case they have been sprayed.

450 g (1 lb) carrots, scrubbed and coarsely grated
2 medium-sized, tart eating apples (1½ apples cored and
finely chopped, ½ apple thinly sliced)
25 g (1 oz) sultanas, soaked for one hour in 15 ml
(1 tablespoon) lemon juice
10 ml (2 teaspoons) French mustard
30 ml (2 tablespoons) olive oil
salt and black pepper to taste

Combine the carrot, chopped apple, sultanas (reserving 5 ml/ 1 teaspoon) and lemon juice in a serving bowl and mix well together. Beat the oil into the mustard and pour the mixture over the salad. Add salt and black pepper to taste.

Toss the salad well, garnish with the apple rings and sprinkle the reserved sultanas over the top.

Tomato, Apple and Watercress Salad

A simple but colourful late summer, autumn or winter salad which makes a good starter or side salad. For a late summer salad try Howgate apples, for autumn, James Grieves and in the winter months, Bramleys.

1 bunch watercress, coarsely shredded
½ medium cooking apple, or 1 eating apple, cored and
chopped
15 ml (1 tablespoon) lemon juice
salt and black pepper to taste
225 g (8 oz) firm tomatoes, sliced
100 ml (4 fl oz) Mayonnaise (see page 154)

Combine the watercress with the apples, toss the mixture in the lemon juice and season it with salt and black pepper. Arrange the tomatoes in the bottom of a serving bowl and salt and pepper them to taste.

Pile the apple and watercress on top and serve the salad with a separate bowl of mayonnaise.

Tomatoes with Basil

No herb has a greater affinity – or is it love? – for a vegetable (or is it a fruit?) than basil for tomato. Given ideal conditions, and they did occur on quite a few occasions last summer, we would use fleshy Italian plum tomatoes, broad-leaved sweet basil, mild Spanish onions and the tiny, flavourful Little Gem Cos lettuce which can be bought in certain stores, or home-grown. We would never grow tired of this salad if we had to eat it every day.

500 g (1 lb) tomatoes, cut lengthwise into six
1 medium onion, finely chopped
6–8 leaves basil, lightly torn
salt and pepper to taste
15 ml (1 tablespoon) olive oil
5 ml (1 teaspoon) vinegar
heart of 1 small Cos lettuce
10 ml (2 teaspoons) walnut oil
black olives to garnish

Place the tomatoes, onion and basil in a mixing bowl. Season to taste with salt and pepper. Toss lightly together and pile in the centre of a large, decorative serving plate.

Dribble the olive oil and the vinegar over the salad. Casually ring the central salad with the separated lettuce leaves. Dribble the walnut oil over the lettuce and garnish the whole salad with a scattering of black olives.

Sweet and Sour Celery and Apple Salad

The salad is lightly dressed in a sweet and sour mixture of honey
and lemon juice and it is at its best with matching sweet-sour
apples such as the Granny Smiths, which are available in late
summer and autumn.

2 medium-sized eating apples, cored and diced
2 sticks celery, finely chopped
30 ml (2 tablespoons) lemon juice
15 ml (1 tablespoon) clear honey
25 g (1 oz) chopped walnuts

Combine the apple and celery in a serving bowl. Pour over the
lemon juice and honey, mix well together and chill before serving,
sprinkled with chopped walnuts.

VARIATION
Replace the lemon juice with double the quantity of natural
yoghurt.

Mexican Cucumber

Towards the end of summer and in early autumn several of our
growers have long 20-cm (8-in), hot, piquant red peppers for sale.
The red *jalapeño* (bullet) peppers, with their unmatchable, nose-
twitching hot peppery smell are also available at this time. You
must not underestimate them. Either sort will enliven a simple
cucumber salad.

If you want a lighter, low-fat topping, replace the soured cream
with *fromage blanc* or Strained Yoghurt (page 159).

1 cucumber, peeled and finely diced

10 ml (2 teaspoons) salt

1 large clove garlic, crushed

30 ml (2 tablespoons) lime or lemon juice

1–2 red *jalapeño* peppers, deseeded and cut into
paper-thin rings

soured cream to garnish

Place the cucumber in a colander, sprinkle with salt and leave to drain for at least 30 minutes. Shake the cucumber free of all excess liquid and turn it into a small mixing bowl.

Add crushed garlic, citrus juice and pepper rings. Mix well and arrange on four small plates. Put a good dollop of soured cream on each plate and serve.

Simple French Bean Salad in Lemon Dressing

Young French beans at their best should be crisp and snap easily when broken in two. They need only a minimum of cooking and the cooked beans should still have some crunch.

450 g (1 lb) young French beans, topped only

salt

60 ml (4 tablespoons) olive oil

30 ml (2 tablespoons) lemon juice

black pepper

50 g (2 oz) black olives (stone and chop 4 or 5 olives, leave
the rest whole)

Put the beans in a large pan of salted boiling water and cook for 10 minutes or less. Drain them, rinse immediately under cold running water, drain again and then put them into a salad bowl. Add the oil, lemon juice, black pepper and whole olives. Toss well and chill slightly before serving garnished with the chopped olives.

VARIATION

For a more substantial salad, add 2 or 3 quartered hardboiled eggs to the salad before serving.

Gingered Beans

A dainty, Chinese-inspired salad whose unusual flavour and texture is achieved by deep frying the beans in oil (like chips). The beans can also be shallow-fried in a sauté pan or wok.

oil for deep frying
600 g (1¼ lb) French or kidney beans, topped and tailed
15 ml (1 tablespoon) vegetable oil
10 ml (2 teaspoons) chopped ginger root
30 ml (2 tablespoons) water or stock
5 ml (1 teaspoon) salt
5 ml (1 teaspoon) sugar
10 ml (2 teaspoons) soy sauce
5 ml (1 teaspoon) vinegar
5 ml (1 teaspoon) sesame oil
2–3 spring onions, finely sliced

Heat the oil for frying in a deep pan. Gently place the washed and well-dried beans in a deep-frying basket and lower into the oil. Remove the beans after 3–4 minutes when the skins have begun to blister. Drain the beans. Reheat the oil to very hot and replace the beans. Cook for 1 or 2 minutes until they have started to turn crisp and brown. Remove the beans and leave to drain again on kitchen paper to remove excess oil.

Heat the vegetable oil over a medium heat in a small frying pan (but one which will take the beans), add half the chopped ginger and cook for no more than 1 minute, stirring constantly. Add the stock, salt, sugar and reduce by one-third, still stirring constantly. Add the drained beans before the contents of the frying pan begin to brown, and then, still stirring, cook off all the liquid.

Empty the contents of the frying pan into a serving dish. Add the soy sauce, vinegar and sesame oil and mix well. Garnish with the remaining chopped ginger and the sliced onions and chill well before serving.

Celery and Banana Salad

Like many a couple, celery and banana make a good marriage because they have such different characteristics. The celery, crisp and slightly bitter, is set against the soft, slightly sweet banana. Dressed up with a light, spicy sauce they make an unusual but extremely tasty dish.

½ head celery, washed, cut into 1-cm (⅜-in) sections
3–4 firm bananas, peeled and cut into 1-cm (⅜-in) rounds
30 ml (2 tablespoons) cumin seeds
5 ml (1 teaspoon) coriander seeds
5 ml (1 teaspoon) cardamom pods
200 ml (7 fl oz) natural yoghurt
salt and cayenne pepper to taste

Put the celery and the bananas in a mixing bowl. Lightly toast the cumin and coriander seeds in a heavy metal pan until they begin to dance. Empty the seeds into a mortar, add the cardamom and grind lightly. Remove the cardamom husks, then add the spices to the yoghurt in a small bowl. Season the yoghurt with the salt and cayenne pepper and stir well. Add the spiced yoghurt to the celery

and banana and fold gently together. Turn into a serving bowl and
serve.

Four-Colour Salad with Japanese
White Dressing

A Japanese-inspired salad which combines different colours,
shapes, tastes and textures in a delicious and healthy way. Serve as a
starter or as an accompaniment to a main meal. This is particularly
good with spiced and/or chilli hot dishes when its cooling,
sweetish flavour is much appreciated.

> 100 g (4 oz) white radish (daikon or mooli), peeled and cut
> into matchsticks
> 100 g (4 oz) carrots, peeled, cut into thin rounds
> 100 g (4 oz) green beans, topped, tailed (string if needed)
> 50 g (2 oz) dried apricots, washed and finely chopped
> Japanese White Dressing [(vinegared variation), page 173]

Par-boil the radish and carrots in lightly salted boiling water for
just 2 minutes. Drain and rinse immediately in cold water; drain
again. Par-boil the beans for 3 minutes. Drain and chill in cold
water; drain again. Combine the vegetables and dried apricots and
stir in the white dressing. Serve on individual plates.

Tabbouleh

SERVES 4 TO 6

This recipe is adapted from one in David Scott's book, *Traditional
Arab Cookery*. Tabbouleh is a Middle-Eastern salad made with
burghul or bulgar (cracked wheat), lots of fresh parsley and mint,
lemon juice and olive oil. There are no hard and fast rules and the

way the salad is prepared depends very much on individual taste.

The recipe given here is a guide and you should vary the amounts used to suit yourself. Tabbouleh can be served as a starter, side salad or main-dish salad. It's also very good as a filling in pitta bread with falafel (Middle-Eastern deep-fried bean croquettes) or kebabs.

225 g (8 oz) fine burghul (cracked wheat)
225 g (8 oz) onion and/or spring onion, finely chopped
2 bunches fresh parsley, chopped
60 ml (4 tablespoons) chopped fresh mint or 20 ml
(4 teaspoons) crushed dried mint
3 medium tomatoes, finely chopped
100 ml (4 fl oz) lemon juice
100 ml (4 fl oz) olive oil
5 ml (1 teaspoon) allspice (optional)
salt and black pepper to taste
wedges of lemon for garnishing

Cover the burghul with plenty of cold water and leave for 1 hour. Drain in a colander and squeeze out any excess water by gently pressing the wheat with your hand (or patting dry in a clean tea-towel). Put the burghul into a large serving bowl and gently stir in all the remaining ingredients except the lemon wedges. Taste, and adjust the seasoning. Garnish with lemon wedges.

Globe Artichoke Starter

Globe artichokes are such a tasty seasonal treat that, provided they are fresh, they are not to be missed. For a dinner party, they make a trouble-free appetizer, the eating of which is bound to unfreeze the most formal gathering since it is quite impossible to eat them in an over-dignified manner. They also give the quieter of your guests a chance to say something while the more loquacious have their mouths occupied. Place a large bowl or plate in the centre of the table for everyone to throw in their discarded leaves and any inedible chokes. This way every guest ends up with a clean plate and doesn't have to make excuses to the host or hostess if artichokes are not their favourite food. Remember, it is the interesting flavour you are serving; there is often very little flesh on artichokes. People certainly don't get fat on them, so follow up with a substantial main course.

Allow 2 small Italian or English artichokes or 1 large Breton artichoke per person and prepare and cook them as described on page 13. Stand the cooked artichokes upside-down to drain and cool.

Serve lukewarm with a choice of dressings. For example: a lemon-flavoured mayonnaise and a vinaigrette dressing made with olive oil and thick cream, seasoned with salt and pepper and sharpened with lemon juice.

Potato Short Eats

Short eats are pungent or sweet snacks of Sri Lankan/Indian origin. They go well with a few drinks or a beer (not, we hasten to add, with fine wines). Do find some excuse to try this salad – it's ideal party food. Spoon out onto very small plates or shallow dishes and eat with a teaspoon before the papadoms or puffed rice have gone soft.

The papadoms, puffed rice and sev (fine potato noodle, deep-fried) are all optional in that they don't alter the taste of the dish. It is still well worth doing without them, but then you miss out on all the different textures and half the fun.

450 g (1 lb) cold boiled potatoes, finely diced

100 g (4 oz) tomatoes, finely diced

2 medium-sized eating apples, cored and finely diced

1 medium-sized onion

salt to taste

30 ml (2 tablespoons) Hot Sweet and Sour Mango Coriander
Dressing (see page 166)

4 crisp papadoms, or 4 crisply fried Indian puris or fried
Mexican flour tortillas, lightly crushed (optional)

50 g (2 oz) puffed rice or Rice Krispies (optional)

50 g (2 oz) sev or lightly broken potato crisps (optional)

juice of 1 large lemon

lightly chopped coriander leaves to garnish

Put the potatoes, tomatoes, apples and onion into a mixing bowl
and season to taste with salt. Stir in the dressing and mix well. Fold
in the papadoms, puffed rice and sev. Pile the mixture onto a
serving dish. Dress with lemon juice and garnish with chopped
coriander.

Spiced Aubergine Salad

This is Paddy's favourite aubergine dish. It's a cooked salad, so
takes a little longer to prepare, but it's well worth the effort.

2–3 medium-sized aubergines (500–600 g/1–1¼ lb)

10 ml (2 teaspoons) salt

45 ml (3 tablespoons) soy sauce

30 ml (2 tablespoons) wine vinegar

15 ml (1 tablespoon) sesame oil

15 ml (1 tablespoon) sugar

15 ml (1 tablespoon) neutral oil for frying (e.g. sunflower
seed oil)

1 large red pepper, cut in medium-sized rings
1 walnut-sized piece fresh ginger, peeled and grated
4 cloves garlic, chopped finely
salt and hot pepper sauce or chilli paste to taste
15 ml (1 tablespoon) sesame seeds

METHOD ONE

Cut the aubergines in half, salt and drain them and then steam them for at least half an hour until they are soft and collapsed. Drain well and set aside. If you have no special steamer put the aubergines in a small metal colander or sieve placed within or across a large saucepan, part filled with water and with the lid replaced.

Meanwhile, whisk together the soy sauce, wine vinegar, sesame oil and sugar and set aside. Heat the oil in a frying pan and lightly sauté the red pepper for 1–2 minutes over a medium heat (it should still be crunchy). Add the ginger and garlic and cook for not more than one minute (if the garlic burns it will become bitter and ruin the flavour), stirring constantly. Combine these together with the soy mixture in a saucepan and bring gently to the boil.

Remove from the heat. Dry-roast the sesame seeds in a heavy pan over medium heat until they begin to dance; remove them to a plate.

Chop the aubergines into rough 2–3-cm (1-in) cubes and place these in a serving bowl, add the sauce and stir well. Allow to cool, chill and sprinkle with the toasted sesame seeds before serving.

METHOD TWO

Bake the aubergines as described on page 14. Remove the skins before cutting into 2–3-cm (1-in) cubes. Proceed with the rest of the recipe as above.

Indian Tomato Salad

A spicy, mint-flavoured tomato salad usually served with curry dishes.

450 g (1 lb) firm tomatoes, quartered
1 small onion, finely diced
175 ml (6 fl oz) natural yoghurt
pinch cayenne
2.5 ml (½ teaspoon) ground cumin
30 ml (2 tablespoons) finely chopped fresh mint
salt and black pepper to taste

Combine the tomatoes and onion in a serving bowl. Stir together the yoghurt, cayenne, cumin and mint; add salt and black pepper to taste. Gently toss the ingredients in this dressing and serve.

Ratatouille

Correctly cooked ratatouille is one of the most delicious and versatile of all vegetable dishes – it can be served hot as a vegetable or warm or cold as a salad. The vegetables should be just tender and bright coloured and the sauce thick. The use of at least two frying pans simplifies its preparation. It is essential to use olive oil, small, firm aubergines and courgettes and to rid the tomatoes of excess liquid.

350 g (12 oz) small aubergines, cut into 1-cm (½-in) slices
350 g (12 oz) small courgettes, cut into 1-cm (½-in) slices
salt

2 medium-sized onions, sliced

150 ml (5 fl oz) olive oil

2 medium-sized red or green peppers, stems and seeds
removed, sliced

2–3 cloves of garlic, finely sliced

450 g (1 lb) ripe tomatoes, peeled, seeds and excess liquid
squeezed out, and roughly chopped

sprig of thyme

15 ml (1 tablespoon) parsley, chopped

salt and pepper

10 torn basil leaves for garnish (optional)

Unless the aubergines and courgettes are very young and firm, salt them and leave them to stand for at least half an hour in a colander to drain the juices out. Rinse, then gently pat the slices dry on absorbent kitchen paper.

Cook the onions in 30 ml (2 tablespoons) of oil over a medium heat for 5 minutes until they begin to soften. Reduce the heat, add the peppers and the garlic and cook gently for a further 15 minutes, or until the vegetables are just tender. Set aside.

Place 30 ml (2 tablespoons) of oil in a saucepan over a brisk heat, add the tomatoes and quickly (2–3 minutes) reduce them to a thick pulp. Flavour the tomatoes with thyme, season with salt and pepper and add them to the onions and peppers. Brown the courgette slices for 6–8 minutes in another 30 ml (2 tablespoons) of oil in a frying pan over a brisk heat, drain and set aside. Brown the aubergine slices in a similar manner in the remaining oil, drain and add these to the courgettes.

Combine all the cooked vegetables and the parsley in a casserole set on an extremely low light. Stir them gently together and check the seasoning. The ratatouille is now ready to serve. It may be served warm, but it is at its best cold. If you have fresh basil available tear it up and stir it in just before serving.

Smothered Salads

There are other ways of serving lettuce than in a tossed green salad. Try one of these recipes:

CREAMY BLUE CHEESE DRESSING

50 g (2 oz) Blue Stilton
100 ml (4 fl oz) single or whipping cream
20 ml (4 teaspoons) wine or cider vinegar
salt to taste
tight hearts of 1 large or 2 small Webb or Iceberg lettuces
15 ml (1 tablespoon) chopped chives for garnish
16 walnut halves for garnish

Crumble the Stilton into a small mixing bowl, add the cream and the vinegar. Gently whisk these together until all but a few crumbs of cheese have disappeared. Salt to taste if necessary. Set aside.

Neatly quarter the lettuce hearts so that the leaves remain attached to the core. Wash them, peeling back the leaves to check that no dirt or insects remain trapped. Shake the lettuce hearts dry and divide them, cut-side up, on four side plates. Pour over the dressing and garnish with the chives and walnuts. Serve immediately.

VARIATION

EGG AND OLIVE DRESSING

100 ml (3½ fl oz) mayonnaise
100 ml (3½ fl oz) natural yoghurt
salt and pepper
½ medium onion, cut into rings

2 hardboiled eggs, peeled and sliced
8 green olives
15 ml (1 tablespoon) chopped chervil for garnish (optional)

Whisk the mayonnaise and yoghurt together. Season if necessary. Carefully fold in the onion rings and the sliced eggs. Divide this sauce between the lettuce hearts and garnish them with the olives and chervil. Serve immediately.

Chinese Greens with Peanut Dressing

This salad is very good with Chinese flowering cabbage (*choi-sum*). This is a green leafy vegetable with a mild flavour and it is most popular with the Chinese. It is available at most Chinese grocery stores all year round. If *choi-sum* is unavailable the same dressing is good with Chinese white cabbage (*baak-choi*).

225 g (8 oz) Chinese greens (*choi-sum*), washed, trimmed if
necessary, tied into bundles
salt
30 ml (2 tablespoons) creamy peanut butter
15 ml (1 tablespoon) shoyu (natural soy sauce)

Drop the bundles of greens into a pan of lightly salted, slowly boiling water for 2 minutes. Drain the greens, separate them from the bundles and immediately rinse them under cold water until cooled.

Chop the greens into 2.5-cm (1-in) lengths. Mix together the peanut butter and soy sauce (add a little oil if the mixture is too thick). Toss the greens in this dressing and serve them in individual deep serving bowls.

Kitchen Garden Salad

This salad is for people who grow a good variety of leaf vegetables.
It has a delicate flavour and is best served on its own as a first course
or after the main dish.

4 handfuls of mixed young green leaves (lettuce, summer
spinach, sorrel, rocket, dandelion, mustard, etc.)
black pepper
pinch of sugar
15 ml (1 tablespoon) lemon juice
45 ml (3 tablespoons) sunflower oil

Wash the leaves and shake them dry in a cloth or a salad spinner.
Try not to bruise them. Pile them into a salad bowl. In another
bowl, whisk together the pepper, sugar, lemon juice and oil. Pour
the dressing over the salad and toss gently. Serve immediately.

Hot Potato Salad

Served still warm, this salad made with very waxy new potatoes is
very good with a smoked sausage such as frankfurters.

700 g (1½ lb) new potatoes
30 ml (2 tablespoons) finely chopped onion
45 ml (3 tablespoons) olive oil
15 ml (1 tablespoon) wine vinegar
salt and black pepper to taste
60 ml (4 tablespoons) chopped fresh chives

Cook the potatoes in their skins, drain, peel and cut them into thick slices. Combine with the chopped onion. Pour over the oil and vinegar. Add plenty of salt and black pepper and 45 ml (3 tablespoons) chopped chives and mix together lightly. Turn the salad into a clean serving dish and scatter the remaining chives over the top.

Cucumber and Cider Salad

A very cool and refreshing salad which looks very inviting with its pale green colour on a hot day. It looks best in a glass bowl.

2 cucumbers, peeled
150 ml (¼ pint) dry cider
45 ml (3 tablespoons) chopped parsley
5 ml (1 teaspoon) sugar
salt and black pepper to taste

Cut the cucumbers in half lengthways and scoop out the seeds with a spoon; discard the seeds. Slice the flesh thinly and put into a pretty glass bowl.

Mix together the cider, parsley, sugar and seasoning. Pour this over the cucumber and chill for at least 1 hour. Toss gently just before serving.

Cooked Pepper and Cheese Salad

A bright orange/red and yellow salad dotted with green. Serve as a first course.

2 large red peppers, washed and cut in half
2 large yellow peppers, washed and cut in half
100 ml (4 fl oz) olive oil
25 g (1 oz) Parmesan or strong Cheddar cheese, grated
15 ml (1 tablespoon) dried breadcrumbs
30 ml (2 tablespoons) capers
15 ml (1 tablespoon) chopped fresh mint or marjoram
15 ml (1 teaspoon) wine vinegar
sea salt to taste

Bake and skin the peppers as described on page 23.

Heat the olive oil in a frying pan and fry the peppers gently for 5 minutes each side.

Cut the peppers in half again and arrange in a serving dish, alternating red and yellow to achieve a spoked effect. Whisk the grated cheese with the breadcrumbs and sprinkle the mixture over the peppers. Sprinkle over the capers, the mint or marjoram and add a few grindings of sea salt. Leave to cool slightly, then pour over the vinegar. Serve straight away or cool and serve chilled.

AUTUMN SALADS

Early autumn offers the salad maker a veritable cornucopia of local produce at a very reasonable price. Nearly all of the native-grown summer vegetables are still available although the season lacks the excitement of newly arrived vegetables. Abundant apples and pears are supplemented by imported grapes and melons and soon by fresh dates, pomegranates and the beginning of the main Israeli crop of avocado pears.

This happy situation rapidly changes. Vegetables cease growing so quickly, become tougher and more fibrous and lose their sweetness as the strength of the sun wanes. The exceptions to this are mature red capsicums and chillies which achieve a rich mellowness not to be had at other times of the year. Autumn winds and damp cause further deterioration, annual plants die back, leaving only the hardy spinach, endive, celery, fennel, drumhead cabbages and the root crops. It is time to begin buying imported vegetables again.

Early autumn

Local French and runner beans are still available, but take care they are not over-mature, fibrous and full of starch. Look out for and buy the semi-dried flageolet beans, preferably those still in their pods. Sweetcorn is still available, but is only worth buying if the husk is still a fresh green and the kernels a pale yellow. Courgettes are still obtainable, but slice and salt them to remove the slight bitter taste they often have at this time of the year. If you have grown sweet basil strip the plants and preserve the leaves in jars in olive oil or make a pesto sauce from them.

Mid- and late autumn

All root crops, celery and watercress are in fine condition. Chinese cabbage (Peking cabbage) is now at its best. Look out for English or imported bulb fennel and endives of all types. Belgian chicory is now much more reasonably priced. Cucumbers, tomatoes and beans will now primarily be coming to us from Spain, but if you want the very best beans you will have to buy the Kenyan ones. As the more colourful vegetables end their season, enliven your salads with fresh dates, kiwi fruit, pomegranates and avocados. If you have a cool, airy place to store them, buy a bag of shallots. They have many uses, not only in salads, and will keep well into spring.

Chinese Cabbage and Pomegranate in Poppy Seed Dressing

While the pomegranate is not essential to this salad, its soft pink or red seeds make a lovely colour contrast with the crisp, pale green cabbage leaves. They also give an added dimension to the sweet-sharp dressing. This makes a delicious alternative to a green salad.

500 g (18 oz) Chinese cabbage (about half a large one),
trimmed
1 pomegranate
150 ml (5 fl oz) Poppy Seed Dressing (page 167)

Wash the Chinese cabbage well, shake dry and remove any discoloured leaves. Slice the leaves across into 1-cm (⅜-in) sections and place these in a large mixing bowl. Cut the pomegranate across laterally and break out the seeds over the cabbage, taking care not to include any bitter yellow skin.

Pour over the poppy seed dressing and toss well. Turn into a serving dish.

Avocado and Red Cabbage Salad

A friend and regular customer who had spent some time in Israel returned raving about this salad, which she said she had eaten almost every day of her stay there. To us, it seemed an unlikely combination, but after being induced to try it we were converted. The secret lies in the toasted sesame seeds which transform this salad.

500 g (18 oz) red cabbage, outer leaves and coarse ribs
removed
2 ripe but firm avocados
30 ml (2 tablespoons) plus 5 ml (1 teaspoon) sesame seeds,
freshly toasted
salt and black pepper to taste
Vinaigrette Dressing (page 152)

Finely slice or shred the red cabbage and place it in a large mixing bowl. Halve the avocados, remove the stones, peel and then dice the flesh before adding it to the cabbage. Add 30 ml (2 tablespoons) toasted sesame seeds, the salt, pepper and the vinaigrette dressing and toss well together. Turn into a serving bowl and sprinkle with the remaining sesame seeds.

Paprika Potatoes

A hearty, robust but good-looking salad – the red and green garnish is very pretty. It makes good use of those tasty, mellow red peppers available in autumn. At this time of the year we would probably use small Maris Peer, Desiree or King Edward potatoes.

600 g (1¼ lb) potatoes, peeled and cooked though still firm
½ medium-sized onion, diced small
1 large sweet red pepper, seeded and finely diced
75 ml (3 fl oz) Mayonnaise (page 154)
75 ml (3 fl oz) natural yoghurt or soured cream
10 ml (2 teaspoons) paprika
pinch caraway seeds
salt to taste
chopped parsley to garnish

Cut the potatoes into bite-sized pieces and turn them into a large mixing bowl. Add the diced onion and all but 15 ml (1 tablespoon) of the diced red pepper. Add all the remaining ingredients except the parsley and stir well.

Taste, adjust the seasoning and turn onto a serving dish. Garnish with the reserved diced red pepper and the parsley.

Cucumber, Kiwi Fruit and Pomegranate Salad

A beautiful-looking, refreshing starter salad. It is served plain – any vinegar or citrus-based dressing would quite destroy the subtle flavour of the kiwi fruit. The sweet pomegranate juice, with that slightly bitter aftertang from the seeds when you bite them, is enough to enhance this delicate salad.

20-cm (8-in) length of cucumber, peeled
salt
4 kiwi fruit, peeled
1 pomegranate

Finely slice the peeled cucumber, lightly sprinkle the rounds with salt and leave, lightly pressed, for at least 30 minutes. Drain off any liquid.

Finely slice the kiwi fruit in a similar manner to the cucumber. Decorate four small plain side plates in a spiral pattern, alternating cucumber rounds with kiwi fruit rounds. Loosely overlap the slices so that the beautiful centre of the kiwi fruit is not obscured. Cut the pomegranate in half laterally, pull the fruit apart and scatter the seeds across each individual salad, taking care not to include any bitter yellow skin.

Curly Endive with Croûtons and Sesame Seeds

SERVES 4 TO 6

We like the sheer untidiness of curly endive. A few leaves curling and twisting in all directions can fill a salad bowl. Its robust bitter flavour is best accompanied by other strong flavours.

1 head of curly (or Batavian) endive, trimmed of all coarse
outer leaves and well washed

60 ml (4 tablespoons) Vinaigrette Dressing (page 152),
preferably made with walnut or olive oil

30 ml (2 tablespoons) whipping cream

1 large clove of garlic, well crushed

15 ml (1 tablespoon) freshly toasted sesame seeds

36 Traditional Croûtons (page 162)

Break the endive leaves off the head and place them in a large salad bowl. Taste the darker green leaves and discard them if they are too bitter.

Beat the vinaigrette, the cream and the crushed garlic together into a smooth emulsion. Pour two-thirds of this dressing over the endive and toss thoroughly until all the leaves are well coated. Sprinkle the toasted sesame seeds evenly over the dressed leaves. Add the croûtons to the remaining dressing, toss them well and then scatter them over the salad.

Sweet Pepper and Tomato Cream Salad

This is as rich as the preceding salad and even more beautiful: green, red and white flotsam in a sea of red. Serve in small portions.

3–4 firm, sweet red peppers, skinned and deseeded
150 ml (5 fl oz) Raw Tomato Sauce (page 160), chilled
75 ml (3 fl oz) whipping cream, chilled
pepper and salt (optional)
5 ml (1 teaspoon) chopped parsley to garnish

Slice the red peppers into ½-cm (¼-in) rings. Place them in a small bowl, add the sauce and the cream and gently stir together. Season the salad, if necessary. Garnish with the chopped parsley and serve immediately.

VARIATION

Remove the centre core and seeds of 4 large tomatoes. Grill them lightly, skin-side up, under a hot grill. Now, turn the tomatoes cavity-side up, season them and repeat the grilling process. Set the tomatoes aside on four small individual plates and stuff them full to overflowing with the pepper and tomato cream salad, add an extra 5 ml (1 teaspoon) of cream to each tomato, and serve.

Our Coleslaw

True coleslaw is not that commonly seen travesty, rough-chopped cabbage, coloured with grated carrot and sunk in a vinegary mayonnaise-type dressing. When making coleslaw, strive to protect the unique character of the drumhead cabbage. No other vegetable has quite that crunch or a heart of such tightly clasped leaves that can be cut into such attractive, slender, corrugated sections. Try these fine-cut leaves tossed with just a handful of freshly grated carrot, a touch of chopped onion and seasoned with salt, pepper and a few caraway seeds. We prefer it without a liquid dressing at all, but by all means, add mayonnaise if you wish. Do not, however, use a plain vinaigrette dressing or the cabbage will very quickly become translucent and unattractive to look at.

A visually attractive salad can be made from the hearts of Savoy cabbage. The leaves are even more corrugated than those of the drumhead and the soft, mid-green colour goes beautifully with the orange of the carrot. Emphasize this by cutting the carrot into paper-thin roundels. This is most simply done with a mandoline or on the fine-slicing attachment of a food processor, but it can be done with a very sharp knife.

½ small white drumhead (450 g/16 oz) or Savoy cabbage,
stripped of all loose, dirty or damaged leaves
2–3 medium carrots, peeled, grated or cut into roundels
½ small onion, very finely chopped
salt and black pepper
10–12 caraway seeds
150 ml (5 fl oz) Mayonnaise (page 154)

Cut away any coarse protruding ribs from the cabbage, cut it into quarters and remove the stem sections. Very finely slice the cabbage quarters into long shreds either by hand or in a machine.

Discard any unattractive-looking sections. Thoroughly combine all the ingredients in a mixing bowl. Adjust the seasoning.

Flageolet Beans in Rich Tomato Sauce

This is vastly superior to anything you can get in tins, and if you really want to, you can eat it hot on toast.

175 g (6 oz) dried flageolet beans, soaked overnight
and drained
250 ml (8 fl oz) Basic Tomato Sauce (page 159)
½ bunch spring onions, washed, trimmed of coarse green
leaves and then finely sliced
1 clove garlic, well crushed
5 ml (1 teaspoon) dried oregano
15 ml (1 tablespoon) chopped parsley
a few fresh thyme leaves
salt and black pepper to taste

Cook the beans in fresh unsalted water until tender (about 1–1½ hours). Drain the beans then combine them with the tomato sauce, onions and garlic. Add the herbs and the seasoning and set aside to cool. Adjust the seasoning when the salad is cold.

Flageolet Bean Salad

This salad is obviously best made with flageolet beans picked direct from the semi-dried pods. Look out for these beans in early autumn though they are rarely obtainable.

For a treat, serve the salad piled in the centre of halves of small Ogen or Charentais melons.

225 g (8 oz) dried flageolet beans, soaked overnight
4 sticks of celery, washed and finely sliced
30 ml (2 tablespoons) chopped spring onion
salt and pepper to taste
150 ml (5 fl oz) Green Dressing (page 158)
sprigs of watercress for garnish

Drain the beans and cook them in fresh unsalted water until they are tender (about 1–1½ hours). Drain the beans and set them aside to cool.

Combine the beans in a mixing bowl with the celery and the onion and season well with salt and pepper. Finally, stir in the green dressing, turn the salad into a serving bowl and garnish with the sprigs of watercress.

Fennel and Grapefruit Salad

It is often the simplest combinations which work best and so it is with this salad. The sharp, juicy grapefruit is a perfect partner for the crunchy, aniseed-flavoured fennel.

450 g (1 lb) bulb fennel, washed and trimmed
2 grapefruits, peel and pith cut away
30 ml (2 tablespoons) olive oil
2.5 ml (½ teaspoon) salt
fennel leaves for garnish

Cut away and discard the hard cores of the fennel bulbs. Slice the bulbs into thin sections and place these in a bowl. Cut the grapefruit into slices and pull these apart over the bowl, letting the chunks fall over the fennel. Discard any skin or other indigestible matter that is easily removed. Add the olive oil and the salt and mix thoroughly. Turn into a serving dish and garnish with the fennel leaves.

Fennel, Leek and Tomato Salad

Leeks make a pleasant change from onions in an autumn salad. From mid-autumn onwards, we find that tomatoes grown in hot climates under natural conditions have much more flavour than those grown closer to home in artificial or semi-artificial conditions. This salad needs good tomatoes and good olive oil.

1 medium-sized fennel bulb, trimmed and finely sliced
2 medium-sized leeks, trimmed and very finely sliced
350 g (12 oz) tomatoes, sliced
60 ml (4 tablespoons) olive oil
15 ml (1 tablespoon) lemon juice
salt and black pepper

Place the fennel, leeks and tomatoes in a mixing bowl. Dress them with the olive oil and the lemon juice and season with the salt and pepper. Toss the vegetables gently but thoroughly together so that they are well coated in the dressing.

Green Bean and Tomato Salad

It is odd that in autumn and winter you can buy tiny French beans superior to those you buy from your local farmer at the height of the season. These fine beans have been airfreighted to us from Kenya. We prefer to use shallots with the beans and tomatoes. You never need many of them and their attractive, pungent flavour is well worth the extra cost over that of frequently bitter onions.

250 g (9 oz) French beans, topped and, if required, tailed
450 g (1 lb) tomatoes, sliced
4 shallots, finely sliced
1 large clove garlic, very finely sliced
75 ml (3 fl oz) Vinaigrette Dressing (page 152)
salt and black pepper to taste

Drop the beans into a pan of rapidly boiling salted water and cook uncovered for 5–8 minutes until just tender. Drain the beans and rapidly cool them under cold running water.

Combine all the ingredients and mix well. Set the salad aside for an hour in a cool place to allow the flavours to mingle. Adjust the seasoning and serve.

Spiced Beetroot and Walnut Salad

Not many years ago, Paddy used to drive regularly from Edinburgh to Liverpool on a Sunday night. With the journey over three-quarters done, it was his practice to stop at a Lancashire pub for one of their home-made hot-pot pies and a pint of Thwaite's best bitter. It was just a penny extra for a rough beetroot and onion salad that always tasted unbelievably good. Hunger and nostalgia must be two of the best triggers of gastric juices. Here is a delicious beetroot salad that requires neither for its enjoyment.

450 g (1 lb) beetroot, cooked and peeled
1 medium onion, finely chopped
100 g (4 oz) walnuts, crushed
2 cloves garlic, crushed
30 ml (2 tablespoons) parsley, chopped, plus parsley for garnish
30 ml (2 tablespoons) wine vinegar
5 ml (1 teaspoon) ground coriander

salt and cayenne pepper to taste
5 ml (1 teaspoon) dried dill weed (optional)

Cut the beetroot into fine slices or large julienne strips. Place these in a mixing bowl and combine with the rest of the ingredients. Mix very thoroughly and check the seasoning before turning the salad into a serving bowl. Garnish with the reserved parsley.

Kaleidoscope Salad

A colourful alternative to green salad with good clean colours and simple flavour contrasts. Once you have the ingredients it is very quick to assemble. Pre-selected and washed watercress and bean-sprouts are available in sealed packets from many supermarkets. We would prefer to use fresh pineapple but the tinned fruit is a fair substitute.

250 g (9 oz) beansprouts, rinsed and drained
1 bunch watercress, washed and drained
2 slices pineapple
1 small sweet red pepper, halved and seeded
a few gratings of peeled fresh ginger root
15 ml (1 tablespoon) shoyu (natural soy sauce)

Place the beansprouts in a mixing bowl. Remove any roots and coarse stems from the watercress. Lightly chop the remaining stems and leaves and add these to the beansprouts. Cut the pineapple up into small chunks over the beansprouts and water-cress so that they catch any juice that runs free. Slice the red pepper into thin strips and add these with the ginger root to the rest of the ingredients.

Spoon over the shoyu sauce. Toss this salad very thoroughly so that all the ingredients become well coated.

Sweet Red Pepper Salad

This salad is beautiful to behold and has a taste to match. It has a rich, powerful flavour and is best served in small quantities. Try serving it as one of several salads and titbits in an Italian-style antipasto or with a plain baked potato and a smothered lettuce salad for contrast. Alternatively try this recipe in spring when there are abundant supplies of economically priced red and yellow peppers from the Canaries.

3–4 firm red peppers, skinned and seeded
8 large firm black olives
1 clove garlic, crushed
30 ml (2 tablespoons) olive oil
15 ml (1 tablespoon) lemon or lime juice
salt and pepper to taste

Cut the peppers into 1-cm (⅜-in) wide strips and place in a small mixing bowl. Cut the olives in half and remove the stones (don't use an olive stoner for this as they pulp much of the olive flesh, although a cherry stoner is less rough). If the olives have tough skins it is a simple and worthwhile task to peel these off.

Slice the olives into small crescents and add them and the remaining ingredients to the peppers. Mix gently but thoroughly, cover and leave in a cool place for at least 2 hours for the flavours to develop. Adjust the seasoning before serving.

Beansprout and Cucumber Salad

This is a very simple but effective Indonesian salad. It contains no oils but the dressing is quite sweet. Replace the sugar with clear honey if you prefer its flavour. For a more robust dish, toss the finished salad with a handful of roasted unsalted peanuts.

225 g (8 oz) beansprouts, washed and drained
1½ medium cucumbers, sliced in half lengthwise, seeded and
cut into matchsticks
30 ml (2 tablespoons) finely diced spring onion
75 ml (3 fl oz) cider vinegar
15 ml (1 tablespoon) white sugar
2.5 ml (½ teaspoon) salt

Combine the beansprouts, cucumber and onion. Stir the vinegar, sugar and salt together until the sugar dissolves. Toss the salad in this dressing and serve.

Cheese Salad with Lime and Yoghurt Dressing

An unusual salad which is very good served with olives, a green salad and crusty French bread. If limes are unavailable use lemon juice.

225 g (8 oz) Cheddar, Gruyère or Emmenthal cheese cut into
1-cm (½-in) cubes
1 large green pepper, seeded and chopped
2 medium-sized tomatoes, quartered
100 ml (4 fl oz) natural yoghurt
juice of 1 lime
2.5 ml (½ teaspoon) French mustard
small pinch cayenne pepper
2.5 ml (½ teaspoon) dried basil

Combine the cheese with the pepper and tomatoes. Beat together the yoghurt, lime juice, mustard, cayenne and basil. Stir this mixture into the cheese salad. Chill and serve.

Moroccan Cooked Salad

Cooked salads are a great favourite in North Africa where they are served as a side dish to a main meal. They keep well and improve the day after preparation. Fresh coriander is essential for this salad.

2 medium-sized tomatoes, quartered
2 medium-sized onions, coarsely diced
½ cucumber, sliced in half lengthwise, seeded and sliced
in rings
1 sweet red or green pepper, seeded and chopped
60 ml (4 tablespoons) water
45 ml (3 tablespoons) olive oil
30 ml (2 tablespoons) lemon juice
2 cloves garlic, crushed
salt and black pepper to taste
30 ml (2 tablespoons) chopped fresh coriander leaves

Put the tomatoes, onions, cucumber, red or green pepper and water into a pan, simmer for 4 to 5 minutes and then set aside.

Beat together the oil, lemon juice, garlic and salt and black pepper. Strain any liquid from the vegetables in the pan and then pour in the dressing. Add the chopped coriander and gently mix. Transfer the salad to a serving bowl and serve at room temperature.

Cottage Cheese Salad

Cottage cheese is nutritious and very low in fat and this salad served with brown bread makes a healthy and enjoyable light meal.

Other fresh fruit, depending on what is in season, may be used in this salad. We recommend seedless green grapes, apricots, peaches, pineapple and melon.

225 g (8 oz) cottage cheese
1 firm eating apple, cored and chopped
1 firm, ripe pear, cored and chopped
15 ml (1 tablespoon) roasted unsalted peanuts (or other nuts)
10 ml (2 teaspoons) poppy seeds
15 ml (1 tablespoon) lemon juice
5 ml (1 teaspoon) clear honey (optional)
salt and black pepper to taste

Combine all the ingredients, mix well and serve.

Marinated Aubergine Salad

SERVES 4 TO 6

Here cooked aubergine slices are marinated for 2 hours in an oil and vinegar dressing and then tossed with tomatoes and cucumber and garnished with yoghurt. It is a salad which needs some advance planning. It has a Middle-Eastern flavour and is good served with pitta bread as an hors d'œuvre or as an accompaniment to mildly spiced rice dishes.

2 small aubergines, sliced
75 ml (3 fl oz) olive oil
50 ml (2 fl oz) wine vinegar
2 cloves garlic, crushed
15 ml (1 tablespoon) lemon juice
5 ml (1 teaspoon) dried basil
salt and black pepper to taste
½ cucumber, thinly sliced
2 medium tomatoes, quartered
30 ml (2 tablespoons) natural yoghurt

Lightly brush the aubergine slices on both sides with some of the oil and grill them under a moderate grill until just browned and tender enough to push a fork through easily. Cut the aubergine slices into quarters.

Combine the remaining oil, vinegar, garlic, lemon juice, basil and salt and black pepper to taste in a bowl and mix well. Add the aubergines while they are still warm. Transfer the bowl to a refrigerator and leave for about 2 hours. Stir in the cucumber and tomatoes, top with a dollop of yoghurt and serve.

Four-Root Salad

Enjoy this salad at its best in autumn when the newly lifted roots are at their sweetest and most tender. Be careful to prepare the celeriac as indicated on page 18. Mustard-flavouring vinaigrette also goes well with this salad.

1 celeriac root (about 275 g/10 oz)
3 medium carrots
1 medium parsnip
2 medium-sized par-cooked beetroot
30 ml (2 tablespoons) chopped parsley
Vinaigrette Dressing (page 152)

Peel, coarsely grate or chop or cut into julienne strips all the root vegetables. Combine the celeriac, carrots, parsnip and parsley and mix well, then gently fold in the beetroot. Turn the vegetables on to a presentation dish and dress liberally with a well-seasoned vinaigrette dressing.

Pasta with Green Garlic Dressing

A simple and substantial salad which is also an excellent way of using leftover spaghetti – though it is worth making at any time with pasta of all shapes. Green garlic dressing is also excellent with lightly cooked cauliflower.

2 cloves garlic, skinned
150 ml (5 fl oz) Green Vinaigrette Dressing (page 153)
½–1 fresh *jalapeño* (bullet) chilli pepper (preferably red)
600 g (1¼ lb) cooked, cold, lightly oiled pasta
salt and pepper to taste
thick cream and lightly chopped parsley to garnish

Liquidize the garlic thoroughly in the green vinaigrette dressing, then add the fresh chilli and liquidize that until it has broken down into small but still visible flecks. Pour the dressing onto the pasta in a mixing bowl and toss well. Taste for pepper and salt.

Divide into individual portions and top each with a dollop of thick cream or Strained Yoghurt (page 159) and a sprinkling of lightly chopped parsley.

Guacamole

SERVES 4 TO 6

Paddy was just beginning to relax after completing a small, pleasant country wedding lunch when one of the guests approached and said, 'Doo tell me what that wonderful green slime was . . . so-oh delicious.' Well, it was guacamole, this Mexican spiced, creamy avocado sauce which can be used as a dip for raw or par-boiled vegetables, to accompany fish and chicken, or for serving as a starter salad with soured cream and corn tortilla chips or fresh bread.

Guacamole quickly deteriorates once it has been made, for avocado blackens in the air. If you have any over, you can extend its life by almost filling a small container with it, adding a stone from the avocado and then sealing the top with a thin layer of oil. When you want to serve the guacamole, pour off the excess oil, discard the stone, and stir in any oil that remains on the surface.

2 large ripe avocados (the flesh soft but not discoloured)

1 beef tomato or 2 large ordinary tomatoes, peeled, seeded, juiced and chopped

30 ml (2 tablespoons) chopped onion (white of spring onions is best)

15 ml (1 tablespoon) chopped fresh green coriander leaves

15 ml (1 tablespoon) lemon or lime juice

1 clove garlic, chopped very finely

1 fresh chilli pepper, seeded and chopped very finely or hot pepper sauce to taste

5 ml (1 teaspoon) paprika (optional)

salt and pepper to taste

150 ml (5 fl oz) soured cream or yoghurt

Peel and dice the avocados and turn them into a steep-sided mixing bowl. Add all the other ingredients except the soured cream, and mix well (but not so well that all trace of the separate ingredients disappears).

Spoon the salad onto individual plates. Top with a spoonful of the soured cream, decoratively stirred in with a single spiral turn of the spoon.

Orange and White Vinegared Salad

SERVES 8

Daikon or mooli, one of the ingredients in this salad, is the traditional Japanese variety of radish. It is pure white and grows to about 30 cm (12 in) in length. Mild in flavour, it is used both fresh (usually grated) as a salad vegetable or garnish, and pickled. Daikon is now grown in Britain and is becoming generally available, especially in Chinese grocery stores.

This is a versatile salad that can be served as an appetizer or as a side dish with the main course, or on its own with drinks and salted nuts. The salad can be served within 1 hour of its preparation but it is not at its best until at least 1 day later. It keeps well (up to 2 weeks in an airtight container in the refrigerator), so it's worth making more than you immediately need.

225 g (8 oz) white radish (daikon or mooli)
[about 20 cm (8 in) long]
2 medium-sized carrots
5 ml (1 teaspoon) salt
75 ml (3 fl oz) rice or cider vinegar
5 ml (1 teaspoon) shoyu (natural soy sauce)
15 ml (1 tablespoon) white sugar

Peel the white radish and scrape the carrots; cut them both into matchsticks about 4 cm (1½ in) in length. Put them into a large mixing bowl and sprinkle with the salt. Leave for 30 minutes and then gather the radish/carrot mixture in both hands and gently squeeze out all the water you can.

Combine the vinegar, shoyu and sugar and add the mixture to the vegetables. Cover and refrigerate. Serve, if you wish, after 1 hour, but the salad is at its best if eaten about 8 hours later.

Ginger and Yoghurt Rice Salad

A filling, but quite refreshing, rice salad.

450 g (1 lb) cooked long-grain rice
1 medium-sized green pepper, cored, seeded, finely chopped
1 stalk celery, finely chopped
50 g (2 oz) roasted almonds
walnut-sized piece of ginger root, peeled and finely chopped
225 ml (8 fl oz) natural yoghurt
salt to taste
paprika to taste

Combine the rice with the pepper, celery and nuts. Stir the ginger into the yoghurt and add the mixture to the rice, with salt to taste. Set aside for about 1 hour in the refrigerator to allow the ginger flavour to permeate the salad. Garnish with a pinch of paprika and serve.

Haricot Bean and Sweet-Sour Beetroot Salad

Any type of cooked bean may be used to make this salad but white beans contrast well with the red beetroot. This is a filling and tasty autumn salad, good with a main meal, but also fine as a light lunch with bread and cheese.

2 medium-sized cooked beetroot, diced
15 ml (1 tablespoon) butter
10 ml (2 teaspoons) cider vinegar
10 ml (2 teaspoons) honey
225 g (8 oz) cooked white beans

salt to taste

30 ml (2 tablespoons) soured cream (or plain yoghurt)

Put the beetroot in a pan with the butter and gently heat through. Stir in the vinegar and honey. Continue heating to melt the honey and coat the beetroot in the sauce.

Pour this mixture over the beans, stirring well; salt to taste and set aside in the refrigerator to chill. Serve dressed in sour cream (or yoghurt).

Hummus bi Tahini

SERVES 6 TO 8

One wonders what it is that makes hummus the favourite small salad of the Middle East. The name is odd, it looks rather plain, the ingredients are unexciting and yet it is popular enough to be found in delis the length and breadth of this country. It must be the taste that gives it such appeal and yet even this is not obvious at first. You dip in your piece of bread, scoop up some hummus and pop it into your mouth. Not bad, you think, and you try some more. You quickly discover that it is quite compulsive, addictive even, and you try more and more and more. That is why in our restaurant we sell gallons of hummus every week. Our recipe is different from the normal ethnic versions, but a great many people have said how much they prefer our version.

225 g (8 oz) chickpeas, well washed and checked for small stones, soaked overnight

120 ml (4 fl oz) vegetable oil

2–3 cloves of garlic

30 ml (2 tablespoons) white wine vinegar

juice of 2 lemons

150 ml (5 fl oz) tahini
plenty [up to 5 ml (1 teaspoon)] of salt and plenty [up to
2.5 ml (½ teaspoon)] of pepper
oil and paprika to garnish
pitta bread to serve

Drain the chickpeas, cover again with unsalted water and simmer, covered, for about 2 hours or until the chickpeas offer no resistance when squeezed between finger and thumb (add more water during cooking if necessary). Drain, reserving the liquid.

Set aside about 24 chickpeas. Pour the rest into a small mixing bowl, add the vegetable oil, garlic, wine vinegar and lemon juice, and mix well. Pour this mixture into a liquidizer and blend at high speed until smooth. If the mixture is too stiff to blend, dilute with a little of the reserved cooking liquid. Return the mixture to the mixing bowl, add the tahini and seasoning and mix well.

Spoon on to individual plates. Make a small depression in the centre of each salad, dribble in the oil and garnish with the reserved chickpeas and a sprinkling of paprika. Serve with hot pitta bread.

Apple and Grapes with Japanese Mustard Dressing

The large black muscat grapes available in early winter and around Christmas are excellent with this salad, which makes an unusual, appetizing, bitter-sweet starter.

We have recently discovered a new variety of seedless black grapes with quite a good flavour, Royal Ruby, which could also be used in this recipe.

225 g (8 oz) eating apples, cored, cut into small chunks
juice of ½ a lemon
225 g (8 oz) large grapes, washed

30 ml (2 tablespoons) Japanese Mustard Dressing (page 171)
5 ml (1 teaspoon) mustard seeds

Sprinkle the apple with the lemon juice and set aside to chill. Cut
the grapes in half and pick out the seeds with the tip of a pointed
knife. Lightly chill the grapes. Toss the apple and grapes in the
dressing and garnish with the mustard seeds. Serve in bowls.

Okra with Horseradish and Soy Sauce Dressing

We find okra difficult to use as a salad vegetable because the mature
pod gets too sticky and fibrous, and this dish is only worthwhile if
you have very young, tender okra. It goes particularly well with
plain grilled or fried fish.

20 pods young okra, washed well, stalk ends trimmed off
(do not expose the seeds)
10 ml (2 teaspoons) prepared horseradish sauce
45 ml (3 tablespoons) shoyu (natural soy sauce)

Cook the okra in a pan of gently boiling, lightly salted water for
3–4 minutes only. Drain and immediately rinse under cold
running water until cooled.

Cut the okra diagonally into 1-cm (½-in) lengths. Divide the
pieces between 4 shallow serving dishes, making a mound in the
centre of each dish. Mix together the horseradish and soy sauce,
and sprinkle the dressing over the okra.

VARIATION

Cook the okra as indicated above and serve with Basic Tomato
Sauce (page 159).

Spinach with Sesame Seed and Soy Dressing

450 g (1 lb) spinach
salt
60 ml (4 tablespoons) Sesame Seed and Soy Dressing
(page 174)

Wash the spinach leaves well. Bring a large pan of lightly salted water to the boil. Add the spinach and cook very briefly. As soon as the spinach droops, quickly drain it and rinse under cold water until cooled. Drain it well again and gently squeeze out excess water. Chop the spinach into about 4-cm (1½-in) lengths. Toss the spinach in the dressing and serve in deep individual serving bowls with the spinach resting in the centre of the bowl.

Fruit and Vegetable Yoghurt Salad

SERVES 4 TO 6

This salad is a versatile side dish which can be served with many types of main-course meals; its sweet refreshing flavour contrasts especially well with hot spicy dishes.

2 medium-sized eating apples, cored and chopped
2 medium-sized carrots, peeled, thinly sliced
1 medium-sized green pepper, deseeded
and chopped
175 g (6 oz) fresh or tinned pineapple pieces
175 ml (6 fl oz) natural yoghurt
45 ml (3 tablespoons) orange juice
15 ml (1 tablespoon) lemon juice
pinch of salt
cinnamon to garnish

Combine the apples, carrots, pepper and pineapple and mix well. Stir together the yoghurt, orange and lemon juices and salt. Toss the salad in this dressing, chill and serve with cinnamon dusted over the top.

Watercress and Pear Salad

Pears go well with peppery flavours and watercress is no exception. Take great care when buying watercress that it is absolutely fresh and that none of the lower leaves are yellow. This tangy salad is a wonderful foil to gratin dishes like cauliflower cheese or baked pasta. The amounts given will make four small side salads.

½ bunch watercress, washed, drained
1 medium-sized ripe pear, quartered and cut across
into 0.5-cm (¾-in) slices
1 head of chicory, leaves separated and washed
10 ml (2 teaspoons) olive oil
black pepper to taste
50 g (2 oz) Blue Stilton (optional)

Combine the watercress, pear and chicory leaves in a mixing bowl. Pour in the oil and grind in about 4 twists of black pepper from the mill. Toss the salad until the pear juices begin to run. Present the salad on individual side plates and, if you wish, crumble over each a little Stilton.

Walnut, Fruit and Red Cabbage Salad

A sweet and sour salad, crunchy and colourful, good with hearty lamb stews. Also ideal as an autumn lunch with a wedge of tangy White Cheshire cheese.

half a red cabbage
60 ml (4 tablespoons) walnut or olive oil
30 ml (2 tablespoons) lemon juice
2 large oranges
1 large eating apple
50 g (2 oz) walnut halves
1 banana

Shred the cabbage finely and toss with the oil and lemon juice. Leave to marinate in the refrigerator for 1 hour. Peel the oranges and separate them into segments. Core and chop the apple into large segments. Peel and slice the banana into thick rings. Add the fruit and walnuts to the cabbage. Toss all the ingredients lightly and serve.

WINTER SALADS

Winter is a time of little change. There is still plenty of choice, however, and now is the time to make judicious use of the store cupboard. Dried beans, cooked pasta, tinned tomatoes, sweetcorn and so on will be used to make hearty nutritious salads. We will be looking at salads that stimulate the appetite for warming meals, and at salads eaten at the end of a meal to leave the palate feeling fresh and clean.

Side salads eaten as a counterpoint to a robust main course are also important. Sometimes, too, we will want to splash out a little and introduce the cheerful colours and crisp textures of vegetables and fruit grown far from our cold and sunless land. We will show you that creating tasty salads in winter is simple, provided you avoid those varieties which are only at their best in the summer. And do not overlook salads as a valuable source of vitamins, minerals, fibre and high-quality protein in our winter diet.

Vegetables to look out for

Home-grown winter vegetables available include potatoes, carrots, red and white cabbage, beetroot, cauliflower, celery and leeks. If the winter has been mild, look out for purple or white sprouting broccoli at the end of the season. Some of the best and some of the less common imports to look for include new potatoes (from the Mediterranean area), mangetout (from Morocco), French beans and courgettes (from Kenya), all the endives and chicories (from Italy and France), calabrese (green broccoli) and Iceberg lettuce (from Spain and Israel) and Cos lettuce, flat leaf parsley and green coriander (from Cyprus).

Remember that oranges, lemons, and avocados are all at their cheapest now.

Green Leaf Salad

Nowadays, there are many leafy green alternatives to the tissue-paper-thin, hot-house lettuce that is so ubiquitous in the winter months. Buy the crispiest lettuce you can find and mix it with the sharper-tasting chicory, bitter curly endive, shredded Chinese cabbage, peppery watercress or young spinach leaves. Also look out for the mild Batavian or broad-leaf endive, red radicchio and lamb's lettuce or corn salad. Buy small quantities of several types of greens (they all keep exceptionally well, if wrapped, in the bottom of the refrigerator) and mix the textures, tones, leaf shapes and flavours.

350–450 g (12 oz–1 lb) green leaves
(e.g. chicory, endive, watercress, Chinese cabbage,
spinach leaves, lettuce)
15 ml (1 tablespoon) wine or cider vinegar
(or juice of ½ lemon)
45–60 ml (3–4 tablespoons) olive oil or other vegetable oil
salt and freshly ground black pepper to taste
½ clove garlic, crushed (optional)

Wash the leaves and drain them well (the inner leaves of some of the close-hearted varieties do not need washing), handling the leaves with care. Tear the larger leaves into small pieces and put them into a mixing bowl. Make the dressing by combining the remaining ingredients and pour it over the salad just before serving. Gently toss the salad and serve.

Walnut oil is expensive but excellent with green salad. Make the salad and dribble a little walnut oil over it. Add even less wine or cider vinegar, toss well but gently, and serve.

Winter Salad Bowl

A colourful and nutritious salad of lightly cooked winter vegetables. The vegetables given are only suggestions and you could use other combinations that suit your taste or according to availability.

100 g (4 oz) small florets of cauliflower
100 g (4 oz) green beans, topped, tailed and cut diagonally
into 5-cm (2-in) lengths
100 g (4 oz) carrots, peeled, cut in half and then into sticks
100 g (4 oz) fresh or frozen peas
100 g (4 oz) cooked beetroot, sliced
1 small head of lettuce, shredded
15 ml (1 tablespoon) lemon juice
45 ml (3 tablespoons) olive oil (or other vegetable oil)
salt and black pepper to taste

Bring a small pan of salted water to the boil and separately par-boil the cauliflower, green beans, carrots and peas for 5–10 minutes or until each is just *al dente* or firm to the bite. (The process can be speeded up by using more than one pan of boiling water.) Drain the vegetables and allow them to cool.

Place the shredded lettuce in a serving bowl and put the cauliflower in the centre of the bed of lettuce. Arrange the green beans, carrots, peas and beetroot around the cauliflower in separate groups.

Combine the lemon juice, oil and salt and black pepper and mix well. Carefully dribble a little of this dressing over each of the clumps of vegetables, reserving about 15 ml (1 tablespoon) of the dressing. Chill the salad for 30 minutes, then sprinkle over the remaining dressing.

Spinach and Apple Salad with Lime Dressing

In the autumn and winter, West Indian limes are sometimes as cheap as lemons, and lime juice is a delicious alternative to lemon juice in a salad dressing. In this salad the sharpness of the lime juice sets off the sweetness of the apple and the flavour also enhances the sometimes harsh taste of spinach.

> 450 g (1 lb) fresh spinach, washed and drained
> 2 medium eating apples, chilled, cored, quartered and
> chopped into small pieces
> 30 ml (2 tablespoons) vegetable oil
> 15 ml (1 tablespoon) lime juice
> salt and black pepper to taste

Remove any thick spinach stalks; finely shred the leaves. Combine the oil and lime juice and whisk well together. Mix the spinach and the chilled apples, pour the dressing over this mixture, add salt and black pepper and toss well.

Coleslaw Salad in Hot Soured Cream Dressing

This is an unusual way of serving coleslaw salad but it's rather nice on a cold winter's day served as a side salad to a main dish or with hot soup and bread as a light meal. The coleslaw can also be heated through in the dressing and served very hot as a vegetable dish.

350 g (12 oz) white cabbage, finely shredded
100 g (4 oz) red cabbage, finely shredded
10 ml (2 teaspoons) lemon juice
1 medium-sized eating apple, cored and cut into
thin matchsticks
30 ml (2 tablespoons) milk
2 medium egg yolks
5 ml (1 teaspoon) prepared English mustard
5 ml (1 teaspoon) honey
15 ml (1 tablespoon) vegetable oil
60 ml (4 tablespoons) wine vinegar
salt and black pepper to taste
30 ml (2 tablespoons) soured cream

Combine the white and red cabbage in a serving bowl. Stir the lemon juice into the apple and then add it to the cabbage.

Make the dressing. Combine the milk, egg yolks, mustard, honey, oil, vinegar and seasoning in a blender or mixing bowl and beat smooth. Transfer the mixture to the top of a double boiler or to a small heavy pan over a very low heat. Stirring all the time, cook the mixture until it starts to thicken. Put a little of it into a bowl and stir in the soured cream. Pour this back into the pan and heat, stirring constantly, until it is very hot.

Pour the dressing over the cabbage, mix well, grind some black pepper over the top and serve at once.

Broccoli with Hot Coconut Sauce

This salad dish, like Gado-Gado (page 149), is Southeast-Asian in origin. For it to be truly authentic, freshly grated coconut should be used, but desiccated coconut is fine. (If you use fresh coconut in this salad remember that coconuts are very perishable and should be kept in the refrigerator and used as soon as possible.)

French beans, carrots, peppers or aubergines or mixed cooked vegetables may also be used in this recipe, so long as the coconut sauce is prepared in the same way. Serve as a side salad to a curry or other spicy meal or as an unusual starter.

30 ml (2 tablespoons) sesame oil or other vegetable oil

1 medium onion, chopped

2 cloves garlic, crushed

75 g (3 oz) freshly grated coconut or 125 g (5 oz)
desiccated coconut

juice of 1 lemon

pinch of cayenne pepper

salt to taste

water or milk

750 g (1½ lb) broccoli or other vegetables (see above)

Heat the oil in a frying pan and add the onion and garlic. Stir-fry until the onion is softened. Add the coconut and continue stir-frying until the coconut is just lightly browned. Transfer the contents of the pan to a blender or food processor, add the lemon juice, cayenne pepper and salt to taste. Switch the machine on and add enough water or milk to form a thickish sauce that will just run easily off a spoon. Pour the sauce into a small pan and heat through gently, stirring; keep hot.

Cut any tough stem ends off the broccoli and divide it into florets. Cook the broccoli for 6–8 minutes in enough boiling, salted water to just cover. Drain and rinse under cold running water until cold. Pour the hot sauce over the broccoli and serve.

Double Beetroot and Apple Salad

Raw beetroot and cooked beetroot have very different flavours and textures and this salad cleverly makes use of both.

1 large cooked beetroot, peeled and grated
1 large raw beetroot, peeled and grated
1 large eating apple, cored and cut into thin matchsticks
juice of ½ lemon
5 ml (1 teaspoon) grated lemon peel
25 ml (1½ tablespoons) vegetable oil
salt and black pepper to taste

Reserve a little of both types of beetroot and mix the remainder with the apple. Add the lemon juice, oil and salt and pepper to taste and toss the salad. Mix the lemon peel with the reserved beetroot and use it to garnish the salad.

VARIATION

Those people who do not care for the taste of raw beetroot could try this salad with just par-cooked beetroot. Cook raw beetroot in plenty of water until the outer skin will just rub off. Now drain them and cool under running water until they are quite cold. The centres remain bright red and crisp while the outer areas are softer and a darker ruby red. Grate the beetroot and continue as directed in the recipe.

Sweet and Sour Stir-fried Salad

The vegetables in this salad are very lightly cooked, mixed with a sweet and sour dressing and then allowed to cool before serving. Don't overcook the vegetables or the finished salad will have no crunch.

30 ml (2 tablespoons) wine vinegar
30 ml (2 tablespoons) clear honey
30 ml (2 tablespoons) tamari or other soy sauce
30 ml (2 tablespoons) groundnut (peanut) or other
vegetable oil
2 cloves garlic, crushed
1 medium onion, finely chopped
2 medium-sized red or green peppers, deseeded and cut
into strips
350 g (12 oz) white cabbage, finely shredded
½ bunch radishes, trimmed and sliced
175 g (6 oz) beansprouts

Combine the vinegar, honey and soy sauce. Heat the oil in a frying pan or wok and stir-fry the garlic and onion for 1 minute. Add the peppers and cabbage and stir-fry for a further 5 minutes. Add the radishes and beansprouts and cook for 1 minute.

Stir the vinegar mixture into the vegetables. Transfer them to a serving bowl and allow to cool before serving.

Two-Colour Cabbage and Tangerine Salad

SERVES 4 TO 6

Colourful, tasty and with contrasting textures, the tangerines give this salad a Christmas look.

100 g (4 oz) finely shredded white cabbage
100 g (4 oz) finely shredded red cabbage
2–3 tangerines, peeled and sliced
30 ml (2 tablespoons) olive or sesame oil
15 ml (1 tablespoon) lemon juice
2.5 ml (½ teaspoon) salt
6 radishes, trimmed and chopped

Combine the shredded cabbage and tangerine slices and mix well together. In a small bowl stir together the oil, lemon juice and salt and pour the mixture over the salad.

Toss the salad gently and then garnish it with the chopped radishes. Serve at once or cover and refrigerate until needed.

Tomato and Green Bean Salad

Sometimes in the winter and spring tomatoes are not very tasty and in this salad we have used a strongly flavoured yoghurt and tahini dressing to compensate. With its bright reds and greens this is a colourful and, with the dressing, nutritious salad as well.

225 g (8 oz) green beans, fresh or frozen, topped and tailed
450 g (1 lb) firm tomatoes, quartered
30 ml (2 tablespoons) freshly chopped parsley
125 g (5 oz) natural yoghurt
15 ml (1 tablespoon) tahini
15 ml (1 tablespoon) lemon juice
½ clove garlic, crushed
salt and black pepper to taste

Cook the green beans in rapidly boiling salted water for about 7 or 8 minutes or until *al dente* or firm to the bite. (If using frozen beans, cook according to the instructions on the packet.) Cool them rapidly under cold running water to retain the colour and texture. Mix the beans with the tomatoes and most of the parsley (reserve a little for garnishing).

Combine the yoghurt, tahini, lemon juice, garlic, salt and black pepper and stir the mixture into the salad until the beans and tomatoes are well coated. Transfer the salad to a serving dish, garnish it with the reserved parsley and serve at once.

Simple Salad Mezze

SERVES 4 OR MORE

Mezze are Middle Eastern hors d'oeuvre. They may be hot or cold, complicated and exotic or simple and quick to prepare, they are always delicious. Here is a selection of ideas for readily available easily made salad *mezze*. Choose three or four and arrange them on individual plates, one per diner. Consider contrasts in colour, texture and taste when making your choice. Serve the *mezze* with wedges of lemon and a small bowl of lightly salted natural yoghurt. No fixed amounts have been given since the amount you prepare of each *mezze* will depend on how many guests you have and how many *mezze* you wish to put on each plate. They should look delicious and tempting but shouldn't be filling, just appetizing.

- Black or green olives in a lemon-and-oil dressing.

- Thin slices of cucumber lightly sprinkled with fresh mint.

- Slices of hardboiled egg, dusted with ground cinnamon, ground coriander and salt.

- Cottage cheese mixed with a little tahini and sprinkled with cumin seeds.

- Fresh, crunchy radishes straight from the refrigerator, with two or three leaves left on.

- Cubes of avocado with vinaigrette dressing, garnished with thin slices of orange.

- Almonds in their skins, sprinkled with salty water and baked in the oven until browned.

- Green beans, lightly cooked, rinsed under cold water until cooled, drained and dressed in lemon juice and oil.

- Fresh or dried dates stuffed with cream cheese.

Mixed-Up Beansprout Salad

This salad is called mixed-up because it has Chinese, Indian and Indonesian origins reflecting the culinary influences that have affected Southeast-Asian cookery. Surprisingly, the mixed flavours work well and the salad is handy to make if you are short of fresh ingredients. For a low-fat salad use the tofu dressing rather than the mayonnaise.

225 g (8 oz) beansprouts, washed and drained
100 g (4 oz) tinned water chestnuts, drained and sliced
100 g (4 oz) fresh (or tinned, drained) pineapple cubes
1.25 ml (¼ teaspoon) ground cumin
1.25 ml (¼ teaspoon) ground coriander
5 ml (1 teaspoon) soy sauce
45 ml (3 tablespoons) Mayonnaise (page 154) or Tofu Dressing
(page 164)
pinch of ground coriander

Combine the beansprouts, water chestnuts and pineapple and mix well. Stir the cumin, coriander and soy sauce into the mayonnaise or tofu dressing and pour the mixture over the salad. Toss well, garnish with a pinch of ground coriander and serve at once.

Parsnip and Date Salad

Parsnips have a distinctive, sweet flavour that harmonizes well with dates, their unlikely companions in this salad. Use fresh dates if they are available, otherwise use dried dates. Rosemary is not used often in salads but here its slightly bitter flavour offsets the sweetness of the fruit and vegetables.

3 large parsnips, peeled and grated
8 fresh dates or dried dates (pour boiling water over them
and drain), chopped
5 ml (1 teaspoon) fresh rosemary, chopped
Vinaigrette Dressing (page 152) to taste

Combine the parsnips, dates and rosemary, add the dressing to taste, toss well and serve.

Orange, Date and Carrot Salad

This exotic salad is inspired by a similar Moroccan salad. It is good both as a starter, or as a side salad for serving with a hot, spicy main dish or as the final course of a meal.

½ small crisp lettuce (Iceberg or Webb's Wonder), washed
2 medium carrots, peeled and finely grated
2 medium oranges, peeled, pith removed, separated
into segments
100 g (4 oz) dates (fresh or dessert), stoned and chopped
25 g (1 oz) chopped freshly toasted almonds
30 ml (2 tablespoons) lemon juice
5 ml (1 teaspoon) caster sugar
1.25 ml (¼ teaspoon) salt
15 ml (1 tablespoon) orange flower water (optional)

Separate the lettuce leaves and prepare a bed of them in a glass serving bowl. Place the grated carrot in the middle of the lettuce leaves and arrange the orange segments around it. Put the chopped dates on top of the carrot and sprinkle over the toasted almonds.

Combine the lemon juice, sugar, salt and orange flower water and sprinkle the mixture over the salad. Chill and serve.

Winter Fig and Walnut Salad

SERVES 6

A colourful, crunchy salad with a tasty and nutritious tofu (bean curd) dressing. The recipe is adapted from a recipe in David Scott and Claire Golding's book, *The True Vegetarian Cookery Book*.

225 g (8 oz) white cabbage, finely shredded
4 medium carrots, peeled and grated
1 small onion, finely chopped
1 medium-sized cooking apple, cored and grated
100 g (4 oz) dried figs, sliced
100 g (4 oz) walnut halves
Tofu Dressing (page 164)
1 dessert apple, cored and thinly sliced
juice of ½ orange

Combine the cabbage, carrots, onion, cooking apple, figs (reserve a few for garnishing) and walnuts (reserve a few for garnishing) in a mixing bowl. Add the dressing and toss the mixture in it.

Transfer the salad to a serving bowl and arrange the apple slices over the top. Sprinkle over the orange juice, garnish with the reserved figs and walnuts and serve at once.

Spiced Egg and Yoghurt Salad

This unusual starter initially looks plain but it is transformed before serving by the last-minute addition of hot, aromatic olive oil which pours lava-like over the surface of the yoghurt.

450 ml (16 fl oz) natural yoghurt, chilled
salt and black pepper to taste
4 soft-boiled eggs, shelled and quartered
2.5 ml (½ teaspoon) dried mint
30 ml (2 tablespoons) olive oil
2.5 ml (½ teaspoon) cumin seeds, finely ground
2.5 ml (½ teaspoon) coriander seeds, finely ground
6 ml (1 heaped teaspoon) paprika

Season the yoghurt to taste with salt and black pepper and divide it between four small plates. Top each plate with the quartered eggs arranged in rosette fashion. Sprinkle the eggs with the dried mint. Keep these prepared plates chilled until serving time.

Put the olive oil in a small saucepan, add the cumin and coriander and bring the pan to a medium heat. Remove from the heat and stir in the paprika. Pour some of the hot oil mixture over each egg and yoghurt salad and serve immediately.

VARIATION

Replace the soft-boiled eggs with poached or fried eggs. This is a good method but slightly more troublesome than that given in the recipe.

Indonesian Rice Salad

SERVES 4 TO 6

This sounds an unlikely choice for a winter salad but all the ingredients are easily available and it brings a hint of sunny tropics to a gloomy winter's day.

50 ml (2 fl oz) orange juice

30 ml (2 tablespoons) sesame seed or other vegetable oil

30 ml (2 tablespoons) soy sauce

salt and pepper to taste

225 g (8 oz) long-grain brown or white rice, cooked and cooled
to room temperature

50 g (2 oz) beansprouts, washed

1 medium green pepper, core and seeds removed and chopped

1 stick celery, chopped

2 spring onions, chopped

50 g (2 oz) roasted almonds or cashews

50 g (2 oz) sultanas, plumped up with a little boiling water
and then drained

100 g (4 oz) fresh or tinned pineapple chunks

Make the dressing. Combine the first 3 ingredients and season to taste. Mix together all the remaining ingredients. Pour the dressing over the salad. Toss well together and chill slightly before serving.

VARIATIONS

- Serve the salad on a bed of greens.
- Add thinly sliced water chestnuts or bamboo shoots.
- Garnish the salad with a little dry-roasted desiccated coconut.

Red Cabbage in Juniper Cream and Yoghurt Sauce

SERVES 6
A colourful salad which goes particularly well with cold meats.

450 g (1 lb) red cabbage
1 sharp, crispy apple
juice of ½ a lemon
75 ml (3 fl oz) natural yoghurt
75 ml (3 fl oz) whipping cream
12 juniper berries, ground or finely crushed
10 ml (2 teaspoons) cider or wine vinegar
salt to taste

Remove any discoloured outer leaves from the cabbage and the bitter core. Now shred it finely (if you are using a knife, use a stainless steel one). Core and dice the apple into 1-cm (½-in) cubes and dress with the lemon juice. Combine the cabbage with the other ingredients, mix them well together and serve.

Stuffed Apple Salad

This is a variation on a Waldorf salad in which the standard ingredients (except the apple) are combined and then used to stuff small dessert apples. The individual salads look at their best if served in small fruit bowls so that the quartered apples are held in a rosette shape with the celery and nut stuffing resting in the middle.

4 red dessert apples, cored and quartered
2 stalks celery, finely chopped
50 g (2 oz) unsalted peanuts
50 g (2 oz) whole hazelnuts
50 g (2 oz) sultanas
100 ml (4 fl oz) natural yoghurt (or mayonnaise)
5 ml (1 teaspoon) lemon juice
15 ml (1 tablespoon) finely chopped parsley

Arrange the apples in individual bowls so that the sides are supported and the apple forms a rosette. Combine the remaining ingredients except the parsley, and mix well.

Divide the mixture between the four apples and spoon it into the centre of each. Garnish with the chopped parsley and serve at once.

Sushi Rice Salad

SERVES 4 TO 6

Sushi is a general word used to describe a variety of Japanese dishes in which the basic ingredient is cooked rice seasoned with vinegar and sugar. In the most popular type of sushi the rice is formed into different shapes which are then topped with a selection of garnishings (called *nigiri-sushi*). Here we make *chira-sushi* or, as it is in translation, vinegared rice mingled with vegetables. This is a substantial salad and it makes a good main course or buffet meal.

350 g (12 oz) white short-grain rice
550 ml (1 pint) water
60 ml (4 tablespoons) rice or cider vinegar
45 ml (3 tablespoons) white sugar
2.5 ml (½ teaspoon) salt
45 ml (3 tablespoons) vegetable oil
1 egg, beaten
15 ml (1 tablespoon) shoyu (natural soy sauce)
1 medium carrot, peeled, sliced into thin rounds
1 medium onion, finely diced
1 stick celery, finely chopped
50 g (2 oz) mushrooms, quartered
10 ml (2 teaspoons) finely sliced pickled ginger
for garnish (optional)

First wash the rice. Wash it well by stirring it vigorously in a bowl or pan in lots of water. Let the grains settle and carefully pour off the milky residue. Repeat the process until the water remains almost clear (this will be a quick process with good-quality rice; it will take longer with loosely packed rice).

Drain the rice and place it in a heavy pan. Add the water, cover the pan and bring to the boil quickly. Turn the heat right down and allow it to simmer for 15 minutes. Turn off the heat and allow the rice to stand for 5–10 minutes. Turn the rice into a non-metallic mixing bowl and set aside.

Combine the vinegar, sugar and salt and bring the mixture to the boil, stirring. Pour this dressing over the hot rice. Turn the rice gently with a wet wooden spoon in one hand while with the other hand fan the rice with a flat pan lid or rolled-up newspaper. This cools the rice quickly and gives it an authentic shine. Set the rice aside.

Brush a large frying pan with a little of the oil. Beat the egg with 5 ml (1 teaspoon) of the soy sauce and prepare a thin omelette in the frying pan. Remove the omelette and cut it into thin strips. Set them aside.

In the same pan heat two-thirds of the remaining oil and sauté the carrot, onion and celery for 2–3 minutes. Set them aside. Heat the remaining oil in the pan and sauté the mushrooms for a few minutes until just cooked. Remove them from the heat and stir in the remaining soy sauce.

Gently mix the sushi rice with the cooked vegetables and mushrooms in sauce. Transfer the mixture to a serving dish and mould it into a mound. Garnish the top with the strips of omelette and the pickled ginger. Serve at room temperature or chilled.

Three-Bean Salad

SERVES 4 TO 6

This robust salad will keep you well fuelled on a winter's day. The cooked beans are mixed with lots of fresh parsley and this makes all the difference to the flavour of the finished salad. The salad goes well with salami, crumbly tangy cheese, hardboiled eggs and pickled fish.

100 g (4 oz) red kidney beans (soaked overnight)
100 g (4 oz) haricot beans (soaked overnight)
100 g (4 oz) chickpeas (soaked overnight)
4 parsley stalks + 30 ml (2 tablespoons) finely chopped parsley
1 bay leaf
2 sprigs fresh thyme or 5 ml (1 teaspoon) dried thyme
½ medium onion, finely chopped
1 clove garlic, crushed
15 ml (1 tablespoon) wine or cider vinegar
30 ml (2 tablespoons) olive oil (or other vegetable oil)
2.5 ml (½ teaspoon) cumin seeds, ground
salt and black pepper to taste

Drain the beans and rinse them. Put them in a saucepan and cover with (unsalted) water. Bring the beans rapidly to the boil, boil hard for 10 minutes and then reduce to a simmer. Add the parsley stalks, bay leaf and thyme. Cover and cook until all the beans are tender (about 1–1½ hours).

Drain the beans (reserving the liquid for later use as stock) and discard the spent herbs. Put the hot beans in a mixing bowl and add the remaining ingredients. Mix well and leave to cool. Adjust seasoning if necessary before serving.

Use leftover cooked beans or separately cooked beans to make the salad. Tinned beans can also be used for speed. In this case use only tinned chickpeas and tinned red kidney beans.

Spiced Yoghurt and Onion Salad

A very simple, refreshing salad from Sri Lanka, this makes an excellent accompaniment to all those robust English winter dishes such as Lancashire hot-pot, shepherd's pie or cheese and potato gratin.

300 ml (10 fl oz) natural yoghurt
15 ml (1 tablespoon) neutral vegetable oil (such as sunflower
or peanut)
5 ml (1 teaspoon) black mustard seeds
good pinch Madras curry powder
salt to taste
2 medium-sized onions, finely sliced

Spoon the yoghurt into a mixing bowl. Pour the oil into a small pan over medium heat. Add the mustard seeds to the oil and watch closely. Remove the pan from the heat *immediately* the seeds start popping and spluttering. Add the seeds to the yoghurt together with the curry powder and the salt and beat well. Stir in the finely sliced onions, check the seasoning and serve at once.

Russian Winter Salad

SERVES 6

A substantial, mustard-hot salad dressed in soured cream and designed to keep the Siberian cold at bay.

175 g (6 oz) cooked beetroot, peeled and diced
175 g (6 oz) cooked but firm potatoes, peeled and diced
2 medium-sized eating apples, cored and diced
2 medium-sized carrots, peeled and diced
15 ml (1 tablespoon) prepared mustard
60 ml (4 tablespoons) vegetable oil
60 ml (4 tablespoons) soured cream
salt to taste

Combine the beetroot, potatoes, apples and carrots. Stir the mustard into the oil to form a paste. Stir this into the beetroot mixture and set it aside for 1 hour. Just before serving, stir in the soured cream.

Hot Chickpea Salad

Paddy was once served a very basic version of this salad from a vast cooking pot in a Moroccan street market. A steaming ladle of chickpeas, a pointed finger and a nod in the direction of a thick potage of crushed garlic and olive oil, another nod in the direction of a bowl containing a mixture of ground dried red chillies and salt. A primitive, powerful and tasty dish, the essence of which is the rich vapour of olive oil rising from the hot chickpeas.

250 g (9 oz) chickpeas, washed and soaked overnight
1 small onion or shallot
1 small carrot
1 bay leaf and a sprig of thyme
2 cloves garlic
120 ml (4½ fl oz) olive oil
15 ml (1 tablespoon) salt
2 red chillies, diced
vinegar (optional)
chopped onion (optional)

Drain the chickpeas and put them into a saucepan with the onion, carrot, bay leaf and thyme. Cover these ingredients with unsalted water or, if possible, the liquid residue from cooked spinach. Bring the contents of the saucepan to the boil, cover and simmer slowly for 1½ hours or until the chickpeas are tender.

Arrange on the table one small bowl containing the cloves of garlic, crushed and steeped in the olive oil, and another bowl containing the salt ground together with the diced red chillies. Some people may also want vinegar and some chopped onion at hand. Spoon the hot drained chickpeas into four small bowls and let each person help themselves to the flavourings of their choice.

Vegetable and Tofu Salad

Tofu or bean curd is a soya bean product. It is soft and white with a custard-like texture which easily absorbs the flavours of other ingredients. Tofu is now readily available in Chinese food stores and wholefood shops. It is sold in small blocks or cakes and is stored loose in cold water (or in vacuum-sealed packs). It will keep in a container of water for 3–4 days in the refrigerator. Tofu is a rich source of protein, vitamins and minerals.

30 ml (2 tablespoons) sesame oil

45 ml (3 tablespoons) shoyu (natural soy sauce)

45 ml (3 tablespoons) cider vinegar

15 ml (1 tablespoon) water

5 ml (1 teaspoon) clear honey

1 clove garlic, crushed

2 blocks 300 g (12 oz) tofu (bean curd), cut into 2.5-cm (1-in)
cubes

2 stalks celery, finely chopped

50 g (2 oz) mushrooms, washed and sliced

100 g (4 oz) Chinese or white cabbage, finely shredded

Combine the oil, shoyu, vinegar, water, honey and garlic and mix well together. Put two-thirds of this mixture into a large shallow bowl or container and add the tofu cubes. Leave them to marinate in the refrigerator for 1 hour.

Transfer the tofu and marinade to a serving bowl and gently stir in the celery, mushrooms and cabbage. Add the remaining dressing, carefully toss the salad and serve.

Sweetcorn and Kidney Bean Salad

A good, colourful standby for winter that is tasty and simple enough to produce at any season.

100 g (4 oz) dried red kidney beans, soaked overnight
1 medium tin sweetcorn (225 g/8 oz), drained
1 small onion or spring onion or shallot, sliced
salt
100 ml (4 fl oz) Speedy Chilli Dressing (page 162)

Drain the beans, cover them with fresh water, bring to the boil and boil hard for 10 minutes, cover, reduce to a simmer and cook until the beans are tender (about 1–1½ hours). Drain and allow to cool.

Stir the beans, sweetcorn and onion together in a salad bowl, lightly season with salt and then stir in the dressing. Serve at once.

Brown Rice and Bean Salad

SERVES 4 TO 6

Rice and beans are complementary protein partners and, weight-for-weight, this salad has the same amount of usable protein as a piece of steak. Do not, however, think it will be heavy and boring.

The finished salad looks moist, colourful and tempting and, most important, it tastes good.

> 100 g (4 oz) dried red kidney beans (or chickpeas or haricot beans), soaked overnight, then cooked and drained
> 150 g (5 oz) brown rice, cooked, rinsed and cooled
> 45 ml (3 tablespoons) Mayonnaise (page 154)
> 45 ml (3 tablespoons) cider vinegar
> 2 cloves garlic, crushed
> 15 ml (1 tablespoon) lemon juice
> 30 ml (2 tablespoons) finely chopped parsley
> salt and black pepper to taste
> 1 medium carrot, peeled and cut into matchsticks
> 1 green pepper, deseeded and diced
> 1 stick celery, finely chopped

Combine the beans, rice, mayonnaise, vinegar, garlic, lemon juice, parsley, salt and black pepper and gently mix well together. Set the mixture aside in the refrigerator to chill for 30 minutes and to give the beans and rice time to absorb the dressing.

Toss in the carrot, green pepper and celery and serve.

Bean and Pasta Salad

Another excellent hearty winter salad with that protein-rich combination of pulses and grains. Here this combination also provides an interesting contrast in textures.

175 g (6 oz) dried haricot beans, soaked overnight
175 g (6 oz) small elbow or shell pasta
15 ml (1 tablespoon) olive oil
1 clove garlic, crushed
5 ml (1 teaspoon) prepared mustard
60 ml (4 tablespoons) Vinaigrette Dressing (page 152)
30 ml (2 tablespoons) chopped parsley (preferably the flat
continental variety)
2.5 g (2 tablespoons) ground roasted cumin seeds
salt and black pepper to taste

Cook the beans in unsalted water until tender (about 1–1½ hours), drain and set aside to cool. Cook the pasta in salted water until it is *al dente* or just firm to the bite; pour into a colander to drain. Gently toss the pasta to shake any water out of its cavities.

Combine the beans, pasta and olive oil in a small bowl and mix well. Stir in the remaining ingredients and check the seasoning. Serve at room temperature.

Potato and Beetroot with Horseradish Cream

Potatoes are bland and they need assertive companions to put a bit of life into them. The more mature potatoes are, the greater their need for this kind of company. At different times of the year we will have added mint, yoghurt, spinach, lemon juice, sorrel, vinegar, sweet peppers, ginger and chilli peppers and now, in winter, we use horseradish.

700 g (1½ lb) potatoes, boiled in their skins and left to cool
1 medium-sized beetroot, uncooked, but peeled
100 ml (4 fl oz) Horseradish Sauce (page 165) or any
proprietary brand
75 ml (3 fl oz) whipping cream
salt to taste
cream to garnish

Peel the potatoes, cut them into small, bite-sized pieces and place them in a mixing bowl. Coarsely grate three-quarters of the beetroot and arrange over the potatoes. Spoon the horseradish sauce and the whipping cream over the vegetables, season with salt and mix well.

Turn the salad onto a serving plate, top with a dab of cream and grate the remaining beetroot over the salad.

Rice and Lentil Salad

This dish is popular in the Arab world. It is exceptionally nutritious and, like so many peasant dishes, very satisfying. Accompany this dish with a light green salad and a plate of dressed sliced tomatoes.

225 g (8 oz) large green or brown lentils, well picked over,
washed and soaked for 2 hours
1 medium-sized onion, finely chopped
60 ml (4 tablespoons) olive oil
2.5 g (½ teaspoon) ground cumin seeds
salt and black pepper to taste
125 g (5 oz) long-grain rice

FOR THE GARNISH

1 medium-sized onion, sliced vertically into crescent-shaped
slices
60 ml (4 tablespoons) vegetable oil
150 ml (5 fl oz) natural yoghurt
salt and black pepper to taste

Drain the lentils, cover them with fresh water and bring them to
the boil. Reduce the heat and simmer the lentils for 20 minutes or
until they are barely tender. Meanwhile, gently fry the chopped
onion in the oil until it is soft and golden. Add the cooked onion
and the seasoning to the lentils and cook briefly before adding the
rice. Add water to cover and bring back to the boil. Reduce the
heat, cover the pan and simmer for 20 minutes or until the rice is
cooked. Check during this period that there is enough water in the
pan to prevent the rice from drying out. Check the seasoning and
stir the food before spooning it onto a serving dish and leaving it to
cool.

Make the garnish. Fry the onion slices in very hot oil until they
are dark brown and beginning to crisp. Remove and drain on
kitchen paper. Beat the seasoning and the yoghurt together and
pour this sauce into a depression made in the mound of rice and
lentils. Lay the fried onions over the surface of the yoghurt.

Gado-Gado

SERVES 4 TO 6

Gado-Gado is a popular Indonesian salad dish consisting of a
mixture of raw and cold cooked vegetables arranged on a serving
dish. It is served with a spicy peanut sauce which is either poured
over the vegetables or presented separately in a side bowl. It is
light, crunchy, tasty and good for you. The vegetables suggested
in the ingredients list may be changed to suit availability or

personal preference. If you do not like moderately hot food use less chilli pepper than suggested (or omit it altogether) in the peanut sauce.

FOR THE SPICY PEANUT SAUCE

15 ml (1 tablespoon) vegetable oil

1 clove garlic, crushed

½ medium onion, finely diced

½ dried red chilli, seeds removed, chopped or 1.25 ml
(¼ teaspoon) hot pepper sauce

100 g (4 oz) peanut butter

10 ml (2 teaspoons) brown sugar

10 ml (2 teaspoons) lemon juice

225 ml (8 fl oz) water (or the same volume fresh or canned
coconut milk, if available)

salt to taste

VEGETABLES

2 medium potatoes, peeled and cut into even-sized chunks

100 g (4 oz) French beans, topped, tailed and strung, cut into
5-cm (2-in) lengths

2 medium carrots, peeled, cut in half and then thickly
sliced lengthwise

½ medium cucumber, sliced

100 g (4 oz) beansprouts, washed, drained

½ head crisp lettuce, washed, chopped

GARNISH

1 hardboiled egg, peeled and sliced

Heat the oil in a small pan and sauté the garlic, onion and chilli pepper until softened. Put the contents of the pan into a blender or food processor and add the peanut butter, sugar, lemon juice and water or coconut milk. Process until smooth and then pour the mixture back into the pan. Bring the mixture to a gentle boil, stirring occasionally; season to taste with salt and allow to simmer slowly.

Cook the potatoes until just tender, then drain and rinse them under cold running water until cold. Boil the beans and carrots in salted water to just cover for 5 minutes only. Drain and rinse them under cold running water until cold.

Arrange the cucumber, beansprouts, lettuce, cooked potatoes and par-cooked beans and carrots on a serving dish, garnish with slices of hardboiled egg and serve with the hot peanut sauce poured over or in a separate bowl.

DRESSINGS

Included here are all the dressings called for in the recipes in the main part of the book. There are all types – from a basic oil and vinegar dressing to creamier dressings made with tahini, yoghurt, tofu and avocado, to chilli and horseradish dressings and good, old-fashioned mayonnaise.

Starchy salads, particularly those containing beans, benefit from being dressed while they are still warm – this enables the flavourings to penetrate more deeply. Taste and add more dressing, if necessary, when the salads are cold.

Dressings are often the most expensive part of a salad and to add too much is a waste of money. Do make sure, however, that you mix in the dressing well or the amounts we have given may not seem enough.

Vinaigrette Dressing

MAKES 150 ML (5 FL OZ)

Vary your vinaigrette dressings according to the ingredients they are to be served with. We find that heavy, dried bean or starchy root vegetable salads may be best with a vinaigrette dressing with a 3 parts oil to 1 part vinegar ratio, while strongly flavoured greens are best with a 4 to 1 oil/vinegar ratio, and sweet, delicate lettuce is best with a 5 to 1 ratio.

We prefer to use a light olive oil, but its flavour would be wasted if you were going to add strong spices to the dressing, so in that case, use peanut or sunflower oil instead. Mustard is the most usual addition to the basic vinaigrette. It serves a two-fold purpose: first to give 'bite' when used with rich or slightly sweet foods like avocados or root vegetables, and secondly it helps to emulsify the oil and vinegar so that the dressing clings to the salad instead of running off. If you are going to use chopped fresh herbs in the vinaigrette, add them just before you dress the salad.

120 ml (4½ fl oz) vegetable oil

30 ml (2 tablespoons) wine vinegar, cider vinegar or
lemon juice

salt and pepper to taste

5 ml (1 teaspoon) prepared mustard (optional)

Place all the ingredients in a bowl or liquidizer and beat or blend well. Test and adjust seasoning if necessary.

Green Vinaigrette Dressing

MAKES 150 ML (5 FL OZ)

Don't be tempted to be mean with the parsley. The sharp green colour is half the pleasure of this dressing. We find it goes well with starch-rich vegetables such as courgettes or sweet vegetables like tomatoes or beetroot, or with pasta.

120 ml (4½ fl oz) olive oil

30 ml (2 tablespoons) lemon juice

50 g (2 oz) (½ a large bunch) of parsley, larger stems removed

5 ml (1 teaspoon) prepared mustard

salt and pepper to taste

Place all the ingredients in a liquidizer goblet and blend first at medium speed and then at high speed until a smooth emulsion is achieved. Test the seasoning and adjust if necessary.

Mayonnaise

The recent controversy about salmonella in eggs has made many people wary of using raw eggs and indeed, at the time of writing, the government is still advising people not to do so. It is appalling that the Department of Health and the Ministry of Agriculture, Fisheries and Food have tolerated the lax habits that allowed such a prime food source to be contaminated.

If you continue to use raw eggs, take the following precautions:

● Use genuinely free-range eggs from a source you know and trust.

● Store eggs in a cool place and do not keep for too long.

● Never use cracked eggs.

Real Mayonnaise

MAKES 300 ML (10 FL OZ)

The simplest and best method of making mayonnaise is by hand with a traditional hand whisk. There is no mystique about making it. You follow certain rules and in a few minutes there it is, thick enough for a mouse to jog on. Don't dream of buying it. Whatever you make and flavour it with is a matter of personal taste and consideration for the vegetables which it is to accompany. For instance, fine delicate vegetables such as asparagus deserve a mayonnaise made from a light, cold-pressed virgin olive oil from Italy or Provence (method A). Mayonnaise to be thinned with yoghurt for, say, a potato or cabbage salad should be made with the whole egg and groundnut or sunflower oil (method B).

THE BASIC RULES

1. Mayonnaise is much easier to make with fresh eggs.
2. Ingredients and equipment must be warm.

3. Place your mixing bowl on a tea-towel to stop it slipping.

4. At first, add the oil *very slowly* to the thickened egg.

5. Don't use less than 150 ml (5 fl oz) or more than 300 ml (10 fl oz) of oil per large egg.

6. The better the oil used, the less seasoning the mayonnaise will require.

MAYONNAISE A
1 large (size 2) egg yolk
2.5 ml (½ teaspoon) Dijon mustard
a good pinch of salt
300 ml (10 fl oz) Italian extra virgin olive oil or Provençal oil
lemon juice [up to 30 ml (2 tablespoons)] to taste
additional salt and black pepper to taste

MAYONNAISE B
1 large egg
5 ml (1 tablespoon) prepared mustard
good pinch of salt
250 ml (9 fl oz) vegetable oil
wine vinegar (up to 30 ml/2 tablespoons) to taste
additional salt, black pepper, paprika or cayenne
pepper to taste

Put the egg yolk (method A) or break the whole egg (method B) into a bowl or liquidizer goblet, add mustard and salt. Beat or blend at medium speed until the mixture thickens slightly. Still beating, pour in the oil from a measuring jug, drop by drop initially and then, as it begins to thicken, in a slow but steady stream until all the oil is absorbed.

Carefully beat or blend in the lemon juice or wine vinegar and season to taste with the salt and pepper. Store in a cool place, and use within 24 hours.

Mayonnaise Variations

The following are some of the possible ways of giving mayonnaise a different flavour. The amounts given are approximate. They are suitable for use with 150 ml (5 fl oz) mayonnaise.

AÏOLI
2 cloves crushed garlic

CAPER
10 ml (2 teaspoons) chopped capers

5 ml (1 teaspoon) chopped pimiento

2.5 ml (½ teaspoon) tarragon vinegar

CELERY
15 ml (1 tablespoon) finely chopped celery

15 ml (1 tablespoon) finely chopped chives

CUCUMBER
30 ml (2 tablespoons) freshly chopped cucumber

2.5 ml (½ teaspoon) salt

HERBS
30 ml (2 tablespoons) freshly chopped chives

15 ml (1 tablespoon) freshly chopped parsley

LEMON
Add finely grated rind of 1 lemon and use lemon juice (same amount) instead of vinegar in the preparation of the mayonnaise.

SPINACH
3 lightly blanched and finely chopped spinach leaves

15 ml (1 tablespoon) finely chopped parsley

30 ml (2 tablespoons) finely chopped chives

Eggless Mayonnaise

These tofu or soya milk versions are fine as a mayonnaise-like dressing for coleslaw or potato salad, but alone they cannot compare with the real thing.

Soya Milk Mayonnaise

MAKES 150 ML (5 FL OZ)

75 ml (3 fl oz) natural plain soya milk
2.5 ml (½ teaspoon) Dijon mustard
75 ml (3 fl oz) vegetable oil or vegetable and olive oil mixed
lemon juice
salt and pepper
fresh herbs (optional)

Place the soya milk and mustard in a liquidizer and blend until a stable foam is formed. Add the oil slowly and blend at high speed until the emulsion thickens. Add the lemon juice, salt and pepper, and herbs to taste.

Tofu Mayonnaise

MAKES 300 ML (10 FL OZ)

1 × 300 g (10½ oz) tetrapack of silken tofu
30 ml (2 tablespoons) sunflower oil
15 ml (1 tablespoon) freshly squeezed lemon juice
15 ml (1 tablespoon) cider vinegar
5 ml (1 teaspoon) Dijon mustard

salt and pepper
fresh herbs or flavourings of choice

Blend all the ingredients in a liquidizer until smooth. Store, chilled, in a screwtop jar or airtight container.

Green Dressing

TO MAKE 300 ML (10 FL OZ)

This is a good, general-purpose sauce. You can use it on many hot or cold young, tender vegetables and on cold white meats and fish.

1 bunch of good fresh watercress, well washed
15 ml (1 tablespoon) vegetable oil
150 ml (5 fl oz) Mayonnaise (page 154)
100 ml (4 fl oz) yoghurt
salt and pepper to taste
few sprigs of the watercress for garnish (optional)

Trim the watercress of its roots and remove any discoloured leaves. Plunge the trimmed watercress into a pan of well-salted boiling water for little more than 10 seconds. This may seem a minor step, but it does greatly enhance the colour of the finished sauce.

Drain and refresh the watercress under cold running water until it is quite chilled. Squeeze the watercress free of any excess water, roughly chop it, place it in a liquidizer goblet with the oil and blend it to a smooth purée. Mix the watercress purée, the mayonnaise and the yoghurt together in a small mixing bowl. Season to taste with salt and pepper. Garnish with watercress if desired.

Strained Yoghurt for Salad Making

MAKES ABOUT 300 ML (10 FL OZ)

Thick yoghurt is superior to the ordinary type for many salads and very firm yoghurt can also be eaten alone as a small starter: see below. Unfortunately, many commercial yoghurts are often more than 50 per cent whey or watery liquid and they need to be strained and thickened.

To do this, take a traditional jelly bag and pour into it 600 ml (1 pint) of natural yoghurt. Hang the bag over the sink or a large bowl and leave it to drain overnight. In the morning, lightly press the yoghurt and turn it out into a bowl. It is now ready for use. A sieve lined with damp cheesecloth can be used instead of a jelly bag.

Excellent Greek strained yoghurt is now available in many shops and supermarkets.

Strained Yoghurt Starter

Mix into the strained yoghurt some chopped fresh herbs such as chives, chervil, dill, parsley or whatever you prefer or have available, season it with salt and black pepper, dribble over some olive oil and serve as a dip with raw vegetables or with hot pitta bread.

Basic Tomato Sauce

MAKES 250 ML (SCANT 10 FL OZ)

This is a universal red sauce. You can make it in quantity and store it, soften it with cream, heat it up with hot chillies, enrich it with hazelnuts, add aromatic herbs, more garlic, paprika, sherry or whatever you fancy. This sauce is good hot or cold.

30 ml (2 tablespoons) olive oil

1 large shallot or ½ medium onion, very finely chopped

1 clove garlic, peeled and lightly crushed

1 medium tin (400 ml/ 14 oz) plum tomatoes, drained and
roughly chopped

bouquet garni (½ bay leaf, sprig of thyme, 4 parsley stems,
tied in an 8-cm/3-in celery stick)

salt and pepper to taste

2.5 ml (½ teaspoon) fine sugar (optional)

Heat the oil in a medium saucepan over a low flame, add the chopped shallot or onion and the garlic clove and cook carefully for 5–7 minutes until the shallot or onion is soft but not browned. Stir in the chopped plum tomatoes, add the bouquet garni, turn the heat to medium and cook, covered, for 15–20 minutes. Check the sauce during this period and stir if necessary.

Remove the pan from the heat and remove the garlic clove and the bouquet garni. Season the sauce with salt and pepper and add the sugar if wished.

Raw Tomato Sauce

MAKES 300 ML (10 FL OZ)

Use good, fresh, ripe tomatoes for the sauce. The skinning and the deseeding of the tomatoes is essential; but don't worry, it is a much simpler task than many people think.

500 g (18 oz) ripe tomatoes, skinned and deseeded (see page
26)

15 ml (1 tablespoon) wine vinegar

30 ml (2 tablespoons) olive oil

15 ml (1 tablespoon) parsley, finely chopped

5 ml (1 teaspoon) dried oregano
salt and black pepper to taste

Place all the ingredients in a liquidizer and blend at low speed until a smooth sauce is obtained. Use the sauce over delicate vegetables, either as it is or thinned with whipping cream.

Rich Sweet-Sour Chilli Dressing

MAKES 350 ML (12 FL OZ)

This is an excellent, thick dipping sauce for strips of carrot, cucumber, courgette, sticks of celery and florets of cauliflower. The same dressing can be used as a very fine marinade and sauce for barbecued pork ribs.

100 ml (4 fl oz) fresh orange juice
75 ml (3 fl oz) wine vinegar
75 ml (3 fl oz) shoyu (natural soy) sauce
75 ml (3 fl oz) Basic Tomato Sauce (page 159)
30 ml (2 tablespoons) honey
10 ml (2 teaspoons) paprika
1 large clove garlic, peeled
1 almond-sized piece of root ginger, peeled
½–1 *jalapeño* (bullet) chilli pepper
salt to taste

Place all ingredients in a liquidizer, blend at medium speed until the solid ingredients have all been reduced, then blend at high speed for a further minute. Taste and adjust seasoning.

Speedy Chilli Dressing

MAKES 120 ML (4 FL OZ)

This chilli dressing doesn't have the subtleties of the Rich Sweet-Sour Chilli Dressing (see above), but it is fresh, hot and tangy. It is quick to make from items in the store cupboard. Use it on green beans, mangetout, cooked dried beans, cauliflower or broccoli.

2 tinned plum tomatoes, gently pressed free of juice
60 ml (4 tablespoons) vegetable oil
10 ml (2 teaspoons) hot pepper sauce
10 ml (2 teaspoons) shoyu (natural soy sauce)

Pour all the ingredients into a small, steep-sided mixing bowl and beat together with a fork or a small wire whisk.

Traditional Croûtons

Croûtons make good crunchy additions to leaf salads whether they be heavy-leaved red cabbage or light and delicate endives and Icebergs.

You need good firm bread for making croûtons. A single 1-cm (⅜-in) slice from a 1-kg (2-lb) loaf will make enough croûtons for 3–4 people.

Take a 12-cm (5-in) pan and cover it to the depth of 1 cm (⅜ in) with vegetable oil. Place the pan over medium heat. Meanwhile, remove the crusts from your slices of bread and cut into 1-cm (⅜-in) cubes. When the oil has just begun to haze, test its temperature by dropping in one of the bread cubes. It should turn quite rapidly to a golden-brown colour. Rescue the cube from the oil, reduce the heat slightly and drop in enough of the bread cubes to loosely cover the bottom of the pan. Fry gently, turning them once. When the cubes are nicely browned all over lift them out with a slotted spoon and drain them on absorbent kitchen paper. Repeat the process until all the bread is used.

These croûtons are best eaten fresh, but they will keep for a day or two in an airtight container.

VARIATION

Take a French loaf and cut it into 1-cm (⅜-in) slices. Spread both sides of these slices with butter or brush them liberally with olive oil. Or spread one side with thyme-flavoured goat cheese or a mixture of equal quantities of Stilton and soft Camembert or pounded anchovies or anything of your creation. Lightly toast both sides of the bread under the grill and serve.

Cream Dressing

MAKES 150 ML (5 FL OZ)

This rich dressing can be stored for up to 4 days in the refrigerator. Try it on fresh young vegetables like carrots, broad beans, broccoli or new potatoes.

150 ml (5 fl oz) double cream
salt and cayenne pepper to taste
15–30 ml (1–2 tablespoons) wine vinegar

Season the cream to taste with salt and cayenne pepper. Whip it until nice and thick. Stir in the vinegar to taste gradually. Chill and serve.

Tofu (bean curd) Dressing

MAKES ABOUT 225 ML (8 FL OZ)

Fresh white bean curd has the remarkable ability to carry a whole gamut of flavours. Blend it with a little liquid, add your flavouring – be it mustard, paprika, honey, shrimp paste, oyster sauce, whatever – and you have an instant, low-fat 'mayonnaise'.

The central ingredient is so bland that these tofu dressings lack the intensity of flavour we prefer, but they do have a very high protein value and are very cheap to make. Here is a basic dressing: try it on crisp lettuce hearts.

175 g (6 oz) fresh tofu (bean curd) drained
15 ml (1 tablespoon) onion, chopped
15 ml (1 tablespoon) olive oil or other vegetable oil
15 ml (1 tablespoon) water
5 ml (1 teaspoon) lemon juice
5 ml (1 teaspoon) honey
salt to taste

Place all the ingredients in a liquidizer or food processor. Blend together at high speed. Adjust seasoning.

Tahini Dressing

MAKES 400 ML (16 FL OZ)

The most popular Middle-Eastern dressing. Tahini sauce can be poured over almost any fresh or cooked vegetables or served as a dip with hot bread. It is very simple and quick to make. The sauce can be thinned down, if it is overthick, with water or more yoghurt. Tahini paste is produced by finely grinding sesame seeds. It is widely available in ethnic food stores and wholefood shops.

150 ml (5 fl oz) tahini (sesame paste)
150 ml (5 fl oz) natural yoghurt
100 ml (4 fl oz) lemon juice
1–2 cloves garlic, crushed
45 ml (3 tablespoons) finely chopped parsley
2.5 ml (½ teaspoon) ground cumin or
slightly less
cayenne pepper
salt to taste

Combine all the ingredients in a mixing bowl and beat together. Taste for seasoning.

Horseradish Sauce

MAKES 250 ML (9 FL OZ)

Horseradish is powerful stuff. If you are making this sauce entirely by hand you would be wise to peel and grate the root out of doors. If you don't, be prepared for tears. A well-controlled liquidizer with a tight-fitting lid will also make the preparation more pleasant. Horseradish sauce is good with beetroot, potatoes or, less strongly flavoured, with asparagus.

50 g (2 oz) peeled horseradish root
150 ml (5 fl oz) double or soured cream
30 ml (2 tablespoons) wine or cider vinegar
5 ml (1 teaspoon) sugar
2.5 ml (½ teaspoon) salt
2.5 ml (½ teaspoon) mustard powder (optional)

Blender Method Cut the horseradish root into small sections and place it together with the other ingredients in a liquidizer or food processor. Replace the lid firmly, blend first at low then higher speed, as the horseradish root is reduced, until the sauce is smooth. Chill before serving.

Hand Method   Grate the horseradish root into a bowl. Lightly whip the cream and add it together with the rest of the ingredients to the horseradish. Stir thoroughly and chill before serving.

Hot Sweet and Sour Mango and Coriander Dressing

MAKES ABOUT 150 ML (5 FL OZ)

A delicious dressing of Indian origin that teases all the taste buds.

the leaves of half a bunch of coriander, roughly chopped

1 hot green chilli, deseeded

1 clove garlic

1 walnut-sized piece of ginger

15 ml (1 tablespoon) liquid from sweet mango chutney

juice and pulp from 1 lemon

salt to taste

Blender Method   Place all the ingredients in a liquidizer or food processor and blend at high speed until a smooth sauce is achieved. Taste for salt.

Hand Method   Finely chop the coriander leaves and put them in a small mixing bowl. Crush the chilli, garlic and ginger through a coarse garlic press and add them to the coriander. Add the rest of the ingredients. Beat well together and check the seasoning.

Poppy Seed Dressing

MAKES 150 ML (5 FL OZ)

Poppy seeds may not transform the taste of a fruit salad, but they will give it a personality.

100 ml (4 fl oz) neutral vegetable oil (e.g. peanut or
sunflower oil)
30 ml (2 tablespoons) lemon juice
2 onion rings, roughly chopped
5 ml (1 teaspoon) poppy seeds
5 ml (1 teaspoon) cider vinegar
5 ml (1 teaspoon) honey

Place all the ingredients in a liquidizer or food processor and blend at medium speed until the dressing is smooth.

Peanut Dressing

MAKES 350 ML (12 FL OZ)

Serve this dressing hot or at room temperature on cooked and uncooked vegetable salads.

1 clove garlic, crushed
1 small onion, diced
15 ml (1 tablespoon) vegetable oil
100 g (4 oz) (unsalted) peanuts or 100 g (4 oz)
peanut butter
5 ml (1 teaspoon) brown sugar
15 ml (1 tablespoon) lemon juice
225 ml (8 fl oz) water
salt to taste

Lightly brown the garlic and onion in the oil. Transfer the garlic, onion and frying oil to a liquidizer or food processor and add all the other ingredients. Blend to a smooth mixture. Transfer the dressing to a pan, bring to the boil and then simmer over a low heat, stirring for 5 minutes. Use immediately or allow to cool.

Coriander Cream Sauce

MAKES 300 ML (10 FL OZ)

A soft, mellow sauce that's good with eggs, pasta, salads and white fish.

1 bunch fresh coriander leaves
150 ml (5 oz) cream
60 ml (4 tablespoons) neutral vegetable oil (e.g. sunflower or peanut)
30 ml (2 tablespoons) lemon juice
15 ml (1 tablespoon) French mustard
salt and black pepper to taste

Wash the coriander well and shake it dry. Cut away all but the finest stems. Place the trimmed leaves in a liquidizer or food processor. Add the rest of the ingredients and blend well together at medium speed until a smooth green sauce is obtained. Test the seasoning.

Blue Cheese Dressing

These cheese dressings are in many ways similar to the vinaigrette dressings in that no one dressing is suitable for all occasions. You need delicate dressings for delicate produce and robust dressings for robust produce. Here are two extremes. Use or modify them to match your taste and requirements.

A Mild Dressing

TO MAKE 150 ML (5 FL OZ)

Use this on lettuce, celery and chicory.

50 g (2 oz) crumbled Blue Stilton or finely diced firm
Camembert or a mixture of both
100 ml (4 fl oz) single cream
15 ml (1 tablespoon) lemon juice
salt to taste
fresh chervil, chives or dill for garnish

A Strong Dressing

TO MAKE 150 ML (5 FL OZ)

Use this on red cabbage, curly or Batavian endive or par-cooked cauliflower.

50 g (2 oz) strong blue cheese, crumbled: Blue Cheshire,
Shropshire Blue or, best of all, Roquefort
100 ml (4 fl oz) strong-flavoured oil (e.g. olive or walnut)
30 ml (2 tablespoons) wine or cider vinegar
salt to taste
Traditional Croûtons (page 162), toasted sesame seeds
for garnish

In both cases, combine the ingredients in a small mixing bowl and lightly beat them together with a small wire whisk. Taste and adjust seasoning.

Spicy Almond Dressing

MAKES 150 ML (5 FL OZ)

Many eastern countries – Egypt, India and Morocco to name but three – have their dry savoury dips. They vary from country to country, from family to family. Sesame and cumin seeds feature in most of these supported by coriander, chickpeas, hazelnuts, almonds, cayenne and other ingredients. Roasting the seeds and nuts first is most important, it really brings out the flavours; but do take care not to burn them. The mix may be made in quantity as it stores well in sealed jars. Here is a typical mixture.

Serve sprinkled over vegetable crudités, as a dip for bread or just in place of salt and pepper.

The appearance on the table of something unexpected like this, simple yet exotic, can make an ordinary meal into a feast.

45 ml (3 tablespoons) sesame seeds
30 ml (2 tablespoons) coriander seeds
15 ml (1 tablespoon) cumin seeds
30 ml (2 tablespoons) flaked almonds
salt and cayenne pepper to taste

Lightly dry-roast the seeds over a medium flame in a small cast-iron dry frying pan. A French crêpe pan is very suitable. Stir constantly until lightly browned. Set aside to cool. Roast the nuts separately in a like manner. Grind the roasted seeds in a coffee grinder, mortar or briefly in an electric blender. Pour the ground seeds into a small mixing bowl with the toasted nuts and season with salt and a touch of cayenne.

Japanese Mustard Dressing

MAKES 70 ML (4–5 TABLESPOONS)

5 ml (1 teaspoon) prepared English mustard
30 ml (2 tablespoons) rice vinegar or cider vinegar
15 ml (1 tablespoon) shoyu (natural soy sauce)
5–10 ml (1–2 teaspoons) sugar

Combine the mustard, vinegar and soy sauce in a small mixing bowl, add sugar to taste and stir well to dissolve the sugar.

Coconut Dressing

MAKES 225 ML (8 FL OZ)

A Southeast-Asian dressing which is good on both cooked and uncooked vegetable salads.

100 g (4 oz) fresh coconut, grated, or 100 g (4 oz) desiccated coconut moistened with 30 ml (2 tablespoons) hot water
½ small onion, finely diced
pinch chilli powder or 0.5 ml (⅛ teaspoon) hot pepper sauce
30 ml (2 tablespoons) lemon juice

Put all the ingredients into a liquidizer or food processor and briefly pulse the machine to form a homogeneous but not completely smooth mixture.

Avocado Dressing

MAKES 300 ML (10 FL OZ)

Excellent as a dip for raw vegetables.

1 ripe avocado
15 ml (1 tablespoon) lemon juice
30 ml (2 tablespoons) Mayonnaise (page 154)
30 ml (2 tablespoons) single cream
salt and freshly ground black pepper

Halve, stone, peel and slice the avocado. Put the flesh into a liquidizer or food processor with the remaining ingredients. Blend until velvety and smooth. Check the seasoning and use immediately.

Mexican Avocado Dressing

MAKES ABOUT 300 ML (10 FL OZ)

A thick, spicy, hot dressing served on or with chopped raw vegetables such as carrots, young cauliflower, celery, tender courgettes. For a thinner, less filling dressing omit the boiled egg. For a milder or hotter dressing adjust the amount of hot pepper sauce used.

1 hardboiled egg, shelled
100 ml (4 fl oz) olive oil
45 ml (3 tablespoons) white wine vinegar
15 ml (1 tablespoon) tomato purée
2.5 ml (½ teaspoon) hot pepper sauce
salt to taste

Put the flesh of the avocado and the remaining ingredients into a liquidizer or food processor and blend until the dressing is smooth.

Japanese White Dressing

MAKES 150 ML (5 FL OZ)

This has the consistency of mayonnaise and is used in Japanese cuisine as a dressing for raw and cooked salads. Make the dressing as needed; it doesn't keep well.

150 g (5 oz) cake of tofu (bean curd)
30 ml (2 tablespoons) sesame seeds
15 ml (1 tablespoon) white sugar
2.5 ml (½ teaspoon) salt

Remove excess water from the tofu in order to get a dressing of the right consistency. Wrap the tofu in 2 or 3 layers of absorbent kitchen paper and place a small bowl containing water on top of it. Leave for 30 minutes and then mash the pressed tofu in a bowl. Dry-roast the sesame seeds over a moderate heat until they are brown.

Crush the seeds into a paste with a pestle and mortar and stir the paste into the tofu. Add the sugar and salt and stir into a smooth consistency.

VARIATION

• The crushed sesame paste may be replaced by tahini or Chinese sesame paste.

• For vinegared white dressing, stir in 10 ml (2 teaspoons) rice or cider vinegar.

Ginger and Soy Sauce Dressing

MAKES 225 ML (8 FL OZ)

A low-fat dressing for serving with lightly cooked vegetable salads, rice and bean salads and root vegetable salads.

15 ml (1 tablespoon) peanut, sesame or other vegetable oil
15 ml (1 tablespoon) finely grated ginger root
100 ml (4 fl oz) shoyu (natural soy sauce)
100 ml (4 fl oz) water
15 ml (1 tablespoon) cider vinegar
1 clove garlic, crushed

Combine the ingredients, mix well together and leave to stand for 15–20 minutes before serving.

Sesame Seed and Soy Dressing

MAKES 100 ML (4 FL OZ)

The basic method given here is for a sweet-and-sour-flavoured dressing, best with crunchy, flavoursome vegetables, while the variation, below, gives a nuttier-tasting, thicker dressing which goes well with softer cooked vegetables such as aubergines and courgettes. Tahini or Chinese sesame paste may be used in place of the sesame seeds.

60 ml (4 tablespoons) sesame seeds
5 ml (1 teaspoon) sugar
10 ml (2 teaspoons) shoyu (natural soy sauce)
30 ml (2 tablespoons) water or stock
15 ml (1 tablespoon) rice vinegar or cider vinegar

Dry-roast the sesame seeds over a moderate heat until they are golden brown. Crush the seeds into a paste with a pestle and mortar. Combine the paste with the remaining ingredients and mix well to dissolve the sugar.

VARIATION
60 ml (4 tablespoons) sesame seeds
60 ml (4 tablespoons) shoyu (natural soy sauce)

Dry-roast and crush the sesame seeds as described above. Combine the sesame paste with the shoyu and mix well.

INDEX